Jill Carter works as a natural health practitioner in Somerset. She is a State Registered Nurse and practises healing, therapeutic massage, acupressure and aromatherapy, and offers dietary and nutritional counselling.

Alison Edwards set up the Polden Naturopathic Centre in Somerset over 20 years ago. She is a State Registered Nurse and a practitioner of complementary medicine, and acts as consultant to clinics throughout Britain and overseas.

The Elimination Diet Cookbook

A 28-day plan for detecting allergies

Jill Carter and Alison Edwards

ELEMENT

Shaftesbury, Dorset ● Rockport, Massachusetts
Brisbane, Queensland

First published in Great Britain in 1997 by
Element Books Limited
Shaftesbury, Dorset SP7 8BP

Published in the USA in 1997 by
Element Books, Inc.
PO Box 830, Rockport, MA 01966

Published in Australia in 1997 by
Element Books Limited
for Jacaranda Wiley Limited
33 Park Road, Milton, Brisbane 4064

Cover design by Peter Bridgewater
Text illustrations by Mary Stubberfield
Designed and typeset by Linda Reed and Joss Nizan
Printed and bound in UK by Briddles Ltd,
Guildford & Kings Lyn

British Library Cataloguing in Publication
data available

Library of Congress Cataloging in Publication
data available

ISBN 1–85230–946–6

Contents

Introduction

Poised on the threshold of change, your mind whirls as you think of those favourite foods you love and crave – the chocolates, the pizzas, the ice-creams and the take-aways. Could there really be some 'hidden enemy' lurking among such delicacies? Could just a simple food allergy have been spoiling your life all these years? Could you reduce your dependency on painkillers, antacids and all those other palliative medicines, just by altering your diet?

The answer quite simply is yes. This book will explain how food allergies can affect you and will then show you how to alleviate these effects. It will guide you step-by-step through an elimination diet, providing recipes for each meal. This will enable you to discover the hidden culprits that are preventing you from feeling really well.

With delicious and nourishing recipes for you to experiment with and enjoy, this book will give you the chance to sample foods that you may never have thought to try before.

There is good news for weight-watchers too. Eliminating food allergies could be the critical move needed to lose those extra pounds or, if you are underweight, to establishing your ideal weight.

If you have been a migraine, eczema or asthma sufferer for years; if you are experiencing pain and stiffness creeping into muscles and joints; if you have digestive problems or if you suffer from depression, mood changes and fatigue; if you have sinus problems, earache, tinnitus or permanent catarrh; if your child is overactive and unable to sleep; or if you have any of the symptoms listed in the next chapter, then this book could provide a solution and be a major step towards enhancing not only your own health but also the health of others around you.

Jack, aged six, was constantly bothered by weeping eczema. Twice he was admitted to hospital as a toddler and on one occasion he had scratched himself so badly that he had to be sedated. Then his mother discovered he was intolerant to all dairy produce and all pulses. Almost overnight he started to improve. For the first time since he was born he started to sleep through the night, his yellow sores disappeared and he became a different child.

Penny had been taking various anti-inflammatory medicines and aspirin for several years for rheumatoid arthritis. However, she then discovered that she was allergic to all dairy produce and citrus fruit. Simply by avoiding these foods, her arthritis has improved remarkably; she has been able to stop her medication, she has not had any severe attacks in her hands, wrists or feet and the swellings in the joints, which had been increasing over the years, have now completely subsided. Now nearly a year later she can forget that she ever had the disease.

CHAPTER 1
An Understanding of Allergies

It is useful to understand exactly what allergies are, the way they can affect you and their possible causes. The word 'allergy' has become a catchword, particularly in connection with food. What we are usually talking about, though, is a food intolerance rather than an allergy.

If you were to have a 'true' allergic reaction to a food, you would know about it immediately as the initial response can be very dramatic. With this type of abnormal hypersensitivity, your body's defence mechanisms would be alerted. Hives, rashes and puffy eyes could appear within seconds; an asthmatic attack, swelling of joints, vomiting and nausea could then follow and, in some severe cases, an anaphylactic shock or an apparent heart attack. Classic foods which cause this type of reaction are shellfish, strawberries, cashew nuts and peanuts. If you are allergic to something, a reaction will occur each time that particular food is eaten. The condition is well recognized by doctors and laboratory tests can confirm the culprits. The problem is then overcome simply by avoiding the offending food.

The words 'intolerance' and 'sensitivity' are both used to describe the other type of allergy, the existence of which orthodox medicine now recognizes. According to the Royal College of Physicians and the British Nutritional Foundation, 'an intolerance is a reaction caused by a food but the mechanism is not clear'. It seems that an intolerance, like an allergy, may also result from a misdirected response of the body's immune system, but the reactions are less obvious. The immune system, which is designed to protect your body from invading organisms such as bacteria and viruses, makes antibodies which kill or neutralize the invaders. In people with allergies, however, the antibodies attack normally harmless substances such as food. This is when a reaction occurs. As you continue to eat the substance, though, perhaps even two or three times a day, your body will endeavour to adapt. Your reactions will become reduced and the symptoms masked, therefore presenting a far more vague and complex picture – so much so that you may have difficulty associating these symptoms with the foods you are eating.

You will often crave and become addicted to the particular food to which you are intolerant. You can give up anything else, you may say, but not your morning cup of coffee, glass of wine or buttered toast. You may not be consciously aware of your craving, but nevertheless will be regularly topping yourself up with the particular food to satisfy your yearnings. This is because you will usually experience a 'lift' after eating a food to which you are intolerant as your body will be producing large amounts of adrenalin to fight the reaction. However, the beneficial feeling will then disappear after one or two hours. As time goes by, and your body starts to get tired from so much over-stimulation, you will need more and more of the food to feel 'good'. In extreme cases, this process is similar to drug, alcohol and cigarette addiction.

If you continue to subject your body to the food for long enough you can reach a stage of exhaustion. Collapsing over your desk at work, suffering from premature 'burn-out', or simply cutting short your trip around the shops – these are all signs that your body's defence mechanism can no longer cope.

Causes

Allergies and food intolerances are on the increase due to a number of factors, such as pollution. Today, we are exposed to more chemicals than ever before – in the air we breathe; in the chemically-contaminated food, water and prescription medicines we ingest; and in the many toxic substances with which our skin comes into contact. Our daily diet contains pesticides, mycotoxins, dyes, additives and many other chemicals. In addition, heavy metals such as lead from petrol fumes and mercury from amalgam tooth fillings can overload the natural detoxifying pathways of the body, particularly in the liver. The result is that the defence systems of the body become over-worked and over-extended and so, not surprisingly, fail to work efficiently.

Nutritional deficiency can also play a part. The increasing use of chemicals in farming, as well as the transport, processing and storage of foods for long periods, can lead to the decrease of valuable vitamins and minerals in foods. These vitamins and minerals are vital for a strong immune system; and since there is a noticeable correlation between immune deficiency and allergies it is probable that if you have allergies or intolerances, you will be deficient in many vitamins and minerals. This is particularly likely if you eat a lot of refined sugar, milk and wheat as these foods can deplete vitamin and mineral levels. Approximately 48 per cent of the raw molasses extracted from sugar cane consists of vitamins and minerals which are necessary for the body to break down and metabolize the sugar molecules. However, most people eat white processed sugar which has none of these nutrients left, so eating this will actually draw on the body's reserves of minerals and vitamins. Wheat, which is high in gluten, a sticky, glue–like substance, can coat the lining of the intestines and can prevent the proper absorption of nutrients from the diet. Similarly, cows' milk can damage the lining of the intestines as the casein can coagulate in the stomach and form a hard mass.

Sugar and wheat can also encourage an overgrowth of unfriendly micro-organisms such as *Candida albicans* in the gut. Candida is a yeast growth present in and on most people. It is normally controlled by the immune defences and the 'friendly flora' in the intestines. However, when the immune system has been weakened, for example by a chronic viral infection such as glandular fever, or the internal flora has been depleted, perhaps by antibiotics or contraceptive pills, the candida can grow out of control and the condition called candidiasis manifests. This condition affects the mucus membranes and allows undigested food particles to pass through the walls of the intestines and trigger off food intolerances. Parasites, such as *Giardia lamblia*, may also trigger food intolerances in the same way by damaging the intestines and destroying the friendly bacteria.

Another contributory factor to allergies and food intolerances may be bottle-feeding with cows' milk. An infant's intestinal tract is very porous and it takes between six to twelve months before it can screen out the large molecules in substances such as wheat, milk products, fish and egg white; so if a baby is fed on cows' milk or solid food during the early months, its digestive system may not be able to cope. In addition, it will be missing the protective substances in the mother's milk and colostrum, so it will not be able to build up a healthy immune system.

There could also be a possible hereditary cause of allergies. Parents with allergies and food intolerances tend to give birth to children with allergies and intolerances, but whether this is passed on through the genes, or through the placenta via the blood, is not known.

In our society, stress and our poor handling of it can also cause allergies and intolerances. When an individual is under stress, the area around the stomach tightens and the flow of intestinal juices is impaired, so that food cannot be properly digested. This, in turn, can create more intolerances, thus setting up a vicious circle. Certain foods can even exacerbate stress. Caffeine, for example, can cause anxiety, palpitations, irritability and insomnia, and food additives have been proved to cause hyperactivity. Quite often when you feel under stress it is better to consider your diet rather than look for external causes.

In the past, germs determined the pattern of illness in society. Today, this is still true, but in addition we have entered an era of man-made illness in which allergies and food intolerances are increasingly prevalent.

Symptoms

The following symptoms can indicate a food intolerance:

- overweight, underweight, fluctuating weight
- itching or burning skin, eczema, urticaria, dandruff, acne, varicose veins
- cramps, nausea, vomiting, diarrhoea, constipation, bloating, flatulence, colitis, ulcerative colitis, irritable bowel, colic, indigestion, anaemia

- discomfort in the muscles of the neck
- backache, aching muscles or joints, fibrositis, arthritis, tingling in the muscles
- insomnia, waking in the night, poor sleep pattern
- impaired energy, chronic fatigue
- weeping/itching eyes, visual problems, sensitivity to bright lights
- sneezing, sinusitis, runny nose, polyps, post-nasal drip, hay fever, nose bleeds
- ringing in the ears, earache
- sore throat, hoarseness, cough, catarrh, asthma, wheezing, bronchitis, breathlessness
- cold/hot sweating extremities, chilblains, hot flushes
- fast/slow pulse, high/low blood pressure, palpitations, unexplained anginal pain
- dark puffy circles under eyes, constant bruising
- painful irregular periods, PMS, thrush
- frequent urination, bed-wetting, water retention, cystitis, frequent colds or infections, excessive sweating, low blood sugar
- inexplicable fatigue, sleepiness, drowsiness after meals, waking up tired, sleep walking, nightmares, hallucinations
- persistent tension/anxiety/nervousness, panic attacks, poor tolerance to pain
- headaches, migraine, convulsions, blackouts, vertigo, dizzy spells, poor co-ordination
- mental confusion, poor concentration, forgetfulness, depression, blank mind, difficulty in making decisions
- hyperactivity, irritability, aggressiveness, violence
- delayed crawling/walking/talking, learning disabilities
- colic, fretfulness, earache, croup
- inability to delay or miss a meal, obsessional eating, craving a special food, constant snacking, poor appetite
- feeling unwell when specific foods or drinks are missed
- feeling immediately better after consuming specific foods or drinks
- tender gums, bleeding gums, mouth ulcers, cracks in lips, sore tongue
- white marks on nails, splitting nails, striae on skin, dry flaky skin, pale in colour

- excessive hair loss, prematurely grey hair
- little desire for sex
- infertility

Of course, some of these symptoms may have other causes.
Insomnia, for example, could be due to a specific incident
which is causing you stress, or backache could be caused by
poor seating at work. But if you are experiencing many of
these symptoms frequently and severely, and not always for
any apparent reason, you will probably find that allergies
and/or intolerances are the cause. So take note if you have
inexplicable panic attacks, for example, or if you feel irritable
for no reason or have any other persistent problem; by
discovering your allergies and/or intolerances, you may
discover the reason for your symptoms.

Claire, aged 26, was diagnosed as having Crohn's
Disease. She spent months in hospital having various
medicines but her disease became worse. She then
discovered that it was due to milk products. Her pain
and discomfort ceased when she eliminated these
from her diet, but she found that she had to be very
strict about this diet. Even a trace of milk or
anything made from milk brought back her
symptoms. Her next treatment would have been an
operation, though, so Claire was delighted to be able
to avoid this.

CHAPTER 2

An Introduction to the Elimination Diet

Now that you have recognized many of the symptoms of your food intolerances, you can move on to diagnosing them. The Elimination Diet is based on a 28-day plan which will allow you to pinpoint which foods are causing you problems. Having done this, you can then work out a diet which is right for you and so begin to build your body up to full health again.

The Preliminary Diet

You may want to prepare yourself before embarking on the Elimination Diet, in which case, the Preliminary Diet will provide a nutritious and varied diet which will give your digestive system a chance to recover. If you follow this for three weeks you will probably find that your health improves dramatically. This is because you will be eating only fresh, whole foods, and at the same time avoiding all the common allergens.

The majority of people with allergies or food intolerances react to less than five items, of which the most common are tap water; dairy products; wheat and the other cereals which contain substances similar to gluten, namely rye, barley and oats; cane and beet sugar; corn; soya; coffee; tea; eggs; peanuts; shellfish; strawberries; tomatoes, potatoes and the other members of the potato family; onions, leeks and garlic; citrus fruits; apples; food additives and preservatives. So it is most likely that, by following the Preliminary Diet, you will also come off all of the foods to which you are allergic or intolerant. If you feel that this has happened, you can then go straight to Day 9 of the Elimination Diet to work through the remaining foods, eliminating any to which you are allergic or intolerant and adding to your diet those to which you have no reaction.

If, however, you are still feeling unwell, you will probably find that you are reacting to some of the less likely foods. In this case, you will need to test the foods more systematically. This you can do by following the initial part of the Elimination Diet. Then, once you have worked out which foods you have been reacting to, you can continue with the plan to sort out whether there are any other foods which cause you problems.

Anyone who is chronically sick or who knows that they have multiple 'allergies' should start at the beginning of the 28-day plan straight away and, if necessary, take it more slowly by introducing fewer foods each day.

The Elimination Diet

The Elimination Diet consists of a modified fast for four days, followed by a gradual re-introduction of foods. Fasting ensures that the digestive system is rested so that the body can begin to extract toxins from the cells and tissues. A pure fast would consist of taking nothing by mouth except spring water. Many people do this regularly because it makes them feel good. However, as the purpose of this book is simply to clear your body of any possible items which may be causing adverse reactions, you do not need to eliminate all foods. Instead, you can eat foods which are very unlikely to cause any reaction. Only those familiar with fasting should attempt a water-only fast as it could release toxins very quickly, causing intense reactions.

By giving your body time to rest by fasting and cleansing, any food intolerances will start to become 'unmasked'. One of the effects of this is that any reaction to a food when re-introduced will be more acute, so foods that have previously had little or no apparent effect on you may suddenly produce noticeable reactions. It will therefore be easy for you to work out whether a food is causing any problems. Whereas before your body may have reacted only when run-down or under stress, and therefore less able to cope, the clearer your body becomes, the more definite the signs will be. You will also find that you can start to listen to your body and sense what it is telling you. This is an important first step to full health.

Preparing for your diet

Neither of these diets can be followed half-heartedly. If they are to be successful, it is important to take time to plan and prepare. You need time to collect the new foods you are going to use and to find shops to supply you.

Choose a quiet time of the year to embark on your diet, away from Christmas, festive occasions or anniversaries when it could be difficult to stick to your regime. For the week prior to starting and during the time that you are on either of the diets, you will need to keep a food diary. On the left-hand side of the page, make a list of everything that passes your lips, including drinks and snacks. On the right-hand side, write down any reactions or feelings that you experience and record the severity of these reactions on a scale of one to ten.

On starting, it is very important not to include anything else in your diet. Alcohol, coffee, strong tea, cocoa, cola, chocolate, spices or other stimulants, including tobacco, will increase any adverse response which may be occurring. This is particularly important when following the Elimination Diet.

This may seem difficult and time-consuming. However, the benefits to your health and to your life will far exceed any minor difficulties you may encounter. As long as you take the time to buy the right foods and cook them correctly, you will be able to manage this diet easily. In addition, the menus have been designed to allow for making packed lunches if necessary. For example, if you work full-time, you can easily make your lunch either the night before or in the morning and then take it with you to work. The same goes for picnics, travelling, or any other occasions when you cannot eat at home.

It is important to prepare yourself for any possible reactions, especially at the beginning. Do make sure that you start either diet when you can devote time and energy to it, rather than when you are very busy with other things. Be prepared to take it easy if you need to.

Withdrawal symptoms

When you first start either of the diets, withdrawal symptoms
are likely to occur and are usually a sign that the diet is
working. These may take the form of headaches, blurred
vision, nausea, an infection, feelings similar to a hangover or
simply an increase in the symptoms you are trying to reduce.
These symptoms can last for four or five days, after which
time they usually cease and a marked improvement in health
is observed. In the case of long-standing illness, though, you
may have to wait longer. Psychologically, you may feel uneasy
and depressed, lack zest and be quite bad-tempered. Know
that this is natural and that your body is just allowing you to
have a last look at what has been suppressed, smothered and
unacknowledged in the past and is now clearing. Know, too,
that these feelings are only temporary. Do not see them as
bad, but just accept them; be 'still' and allow yourself to feel
them. You will be amazed how quickly they will then
disappear. Having a glass of water, doing some deep breathing
or going for a walk can also help.

You will also find that you will 'react' if you eat something
to which you are allergic or intolerant. Again, reactions vary
from person to person and an individual can experience a
variety of reactions. Different foods, for example, may
produce different reactions which may in turn be affected by
different factors such as stress or pollution. It is worth noting
the various different reactions, particularly as the 'clearer'
your body becomes, the more noticeable the reactions will be.
One fail-safe way of discovering whether or not you are
allergic or intolerant to something is by testing your pulse. If
it has quickened, then your body is reacting. Before eating a
food, rest for a while and take your pulse. Count the beats of
your heart by lightly placing your fingers on the artery on the
underside of your wrist just beneath your thumb for one
minute. Remain resting and take your pulse 15 minutes and
30 minutes after eating. If your pulse rate increases by eight
beats or more you are probably reacting to a food.

To ease symptoms, take one teaspoon of bicarbonate of
soda and half a teaspoon of potassium bicarbonate dissolved
in a glass of water. Potassium bicarbonate is not so easily

obtainable but some chemists may be able to supply you. Capsules of bicarbonate of soda mixed with potassium in the correct proportions can be purchased and may be useful when away from home. A herbal alternative is meadowsweet. An infusion can be made by steeping 25g (1oz; ¼ cup) of herb in ½ litre (1 pint; 2 cups) of boiling water. Strain and use in doses of 75ml (¼ pint, ½ cup).

Removing chemicals

If you have not experienced any withdrawal symptoms and your symptoms are still occurring, or are only slightly reduced, it may be that you are reacting to an environmental substance. If you collect together all the chemical substances in your home and put them in a garage or shed and then find that you begin to feel much better, you can then work out which substances are causing the problems. You may think this sounds a bit extreme, but it is usually well worth the effort.

Bars of pure soap can then be used for washing-up, washing clothes, washing your body and all other cleaning purposes in the home. Pure alcohol is available from chemists' shops for use instead of after-shave lotions, and sodium bicarbonate can be used instead of underarm deodorants. Simple wax and liquid polishes which do not smell can be used instead of solid wax shoe polish. Most water-based paints are safe, but new carpets, furniture, paint, floor waxes and sealants can cause problems, as can air conditioning, gas, oil and paraffin.

Illness plagued Carol from birth. During her early years she was constantly troubled by colds, earache and sleepless nights. Her speech development was delayed and it was difficult to understand her until she was nearly seven years old. Dyslexic problems were diagnosed and several years' extra help at school were required. She then became asthmatic at the age of eight. It was then that she was put on a wheat-free diet. The asthmatic attacks ceased, and no

medication was required. Now, 20 years on she has
never had any further symptoms of asthma. The
dyslexia problems were more difficult to solve,
though, and these persisted throughout her school
years. Eventually, however, she discovered that she
was reacting to numerous foods and chemicals, gas
and other fumes. Having discovered the cause of her
dyslexia, she was able to take steps to avoid the
environmental substances. She then rapidly took
some exams and entered a university. She is now at
the top of her class.

General guidelines for the diets

Choose foods that are natural, whole, pure and unprocessed,
wherever possible buying organic produce and meat from
animals which have been reared in humane conditions. This
will reduce the amount of drugs and chemicals you are
ingesting.

If you buy anything that is packaged, you need to take
great care to study the labels. It is worth noting, however, that
in the UK, labels do not have to declare substances where the
content is less than one per cent. Packets and tins of
convenience food can therefore frequently contain wheat or
other grains, potato flour, milk powder, egg and sugar without
you knowing. The list given in Appendix II on page 130 may
help you.

Avoid buying unwrapped fruit and vegetables that have
been exposed to traffic fumes. Wash all fruit and vegetables
thoroughly, discarding the outer leaves of lettuce, cabbage etc.
You can wash vegetables in 500mg vitamin C powder, or 1
tablespoon vinegar, in a litre of water, to help remove heavy
metals and pesticide residues.

Drink plenty of mineral water between meals, about three
to four litres a day. It is best to buy water in glass bottles, but
if you do have to resort to plastic bottles, never leave them in
the sun or anywhere warm as the chemicals in the plastic
could leach into the water. Do not drink straight from the
bottle unless you are going to use the whole bottle within a

short space of time. The microbes from your mouth can breed quickly!

Your usual prescription medicines can be taken, but try to decrease tablets like tranquillizers and sleeping tablets and avoid all unnecessary drugs. Also avoid all vitamin and mineral supplements as they contain fillers and other hidden substances that could interfere with the diet. If any of your prescription tablets are sugar-coated, you can wash the sugar off.

Choose long- or short-grain, organically grown wholemeal rice, obtainable from healthfood stores or some supermarkets. The rice should be rinsed thoroughly before using and you may want to soak it in mineral water for six to eight hours prior to cooking. This brings it 'alive' and makes it more nutritious.

Use sprouted green, brown or puy lentils. Sprouting greatly enhances the nutrient value and digestibility of these foods. As red lentils have been processed, they will not sprout. They are only good for very young children or anyone who is unable to cope with the high fibre content in sprouted lentils. Many beans, grains, seeds and even some nuts will sprout. When water is added, many of the enzyme and metabolic inhibitors, which are designed to keep the seed from germinating until the allotted time, are washed out. If ingested, these can block our absorption of calcium, zinc and other minerals. The water also activates the germination process and starts the pre-digestion of the proteins, fats and carbohydrates into amino acids, fatty acids and simple carbohydrates respectively. The synthesis of many vitamins also takes place, including vitamin B complex, C and E, and these, together with the mineral content, increase immensely.

Special bean sprouters can be purchased but using a jam jar can be just as effective. Take a handful of the item you wish to sprout, wash it thoroughly and place it in a jam jar. Cover it with about three times as much water, then leave it to soak – alfalfa, linseeds, fenugreek, sesame, pumpkin, sunflower and oats will need at least 6 hours soaking time; beans, almonds and other nuts, wheat, rice, millet and rye will need at least 12 hours. Stretch a piece of muslin over the top of the jar and hold it in place with an elastic band. Drain and rinse the seeds through the muslin, then place the jar on its side in a dark, airy cupboard. Repeat this twice a day for three to five days. For the last two days, place the jar in sunlight, keeping the sprouts moist while they grow green with chlorophyll. Refrigerate the sprouted seeds in a covered container and use them raw in salads, soups, etc. It is beneficial to sprout beans for two to three days prior to cooking. Many people who have difficulty digesting beans will find they can tolerate them when they are prepared in this way.

The best way to cook vegetables is to steam or boil them in a little water. Any left-over water can be used as stock or simply drunk as it will contain many nutrients.

Avoid all foods containing additives, preservatives and colourings, including margarines. Although we need to have plenty of poly-unsaturated oil in our diet, margarines are not a good source of this as the oil needs to be fresh, organically produced, and cold-pressed. If possible, buy oil in glass bottles and refrigerate it once opened.

Great care needs to be taken when cooking with oil. Both fats and oils can produce very toxic substances if over-heated or if exposed to light or air for any length of time. This is why lower temperatures are suggested in the recipes. Butter or ghee, pure lard (organic), tropical fats (coconut, palm kernel), sesame and olive oil, in this order, produce the least amount of toxic substances, when heated. If you do need to fry, you can cool-fry by putting a little water into the pan with the fat or oil. When using a wok, use a little water rather than oil.

Sodium bicarbonate (bicarbonate of soda) and cream of tartar are used as raising agents in the recipes. Sodium bicarbonate, which is alkaline and produced naturally in the body, is safe to use. To avoid taking too much sodium, potassium bicarbonate can always be used instead. Cream of tartar also has an alkalizing effect in the body and is safe for the majority of people. It is obtained from grapes so it has been classified with the grape family and is tested in the Prelimary Diet and then on Day 12.

You will notice that foods are introduced according to their food family. This is important because people often react to the botanical 'relatives' of the food to which they are intolerant. For instance, if you are reacting to tomatoes you may also react to potatoes, green peppers, chillies and aubergines. In the case of the grass family, to which most cereals belong, we look more to the subdivisions. Many people only react to wheat or corn, the most commonly eaten cereals, for example, or to the cereals which contain gluten or gluten-related substances, namely wheat, rye, barley and possibly oats.

Whenever possible, sit down and eat in a peaceful and settled atmosphere and give mindful attention to the food you are eating. 'Energy flows where attention goes', so your digestion and your appreciation of food will be greatly enhanced if you do this. Try to chew well and avoid reading newspapers or watching television over a meal, eating on the run, or anything else that might cause stress to the body.

Most of the recipes are designed for four people, as this is the average family size. Even though only one member of the family may be following the diet, it will be of great help to that person if the rest of the family eats the same meal. In addition, the whole of the family will benefit from the diet.

Most importantly, work with good will, love and care when preparing and cooking food. The best food can be marred and ruined for everyone if prepared in a hectic or negative frame of mind.

> As a child, Sally had severe depression and occasional fits. She stopped eating milk products and sugar which relieved the depression and meant the fits occurred only rarely. In her twenties, during a series of exams in a postgraduate degree course, she suddenly found that she could not study. Difficulty in concentrating, severe fatigue and anxiety were all affecting her. A diet of rice, rabbit, root vegetables and bottled spring water for four days solved all the problems and she passed her exams. She then found out that she was reacting to coffee, tea, herb teas, milk products, eggs, sugar, artificial sweeteners and some alcoholic drinks. Since she has discovered exactly which foods she is intolerant to, Sally has never experienced any of the symptoms.

Patricia, aged 35 years, heard that she could lose weight by avoiding specific foods. She found she was intolerant to dairy produce, chemical sweeteners, soya, peanuts and hazelnuts. After an initial period of withdrawal symptoms from sugar and wheat she began to lose weight slowly. She lost 25lb (11kg). Her friends and family were amazed at the change in her weight and health.

Food families

Apple   Apple, pear, quince, loquat, pectin, cider.
Amaranthaceae   Amaranth.
Arum   Dasheen, eddoes.
Aster   Lettuce, chicory, endive, globe and Jerusalem artichoke, dandelion, sunflower, salsify, tarragon, curry leaves, camomile, yarrow, safflower oil.
Banana   Banana, plantain, arrowroot.
Beech   Chestnuts.
Beef   Beef, veal, all cows' milk products. Lamb/mutton, goat and milk products.
Beet   Sugar beet, spinach, Swiss chard, beetroot.
Birch   Filberts, hazelnuts, birch oil (wintergreen).
Bird   All fowl and game birds, including chicken, turkey, duck, goose, pigeon, quail, pheasant, partridge, grouse, eggs.
Blueberry   Blueberry, cranberry.
Buckwheat   Buckwheat, rhubarb, sorrel, amaranth (nearest family).
Caper   Caper.
Cashew   Cashew, pistachio, mango.
Citrus   Lemon, orange, grapefruit, lime, tangerine, citron.
Conifer   Juniper, pine nuts.
Crustacean   Crab, crayfish, lobster, prawn, shrimp.
Cyperacea   Tiger nuts.

Deer   Venison.

Dillenia   Kiwifruit (Chinese Gooseberry).

Elderberry   Elderberry.

Flax   Linseed (Flax).

Freshwater fish   Salmon, trout, pike, perch, bass.

Fungus   Mushrooms, yeast.

Ginger   East Indian arrowroot, ginger, cardamom, turmeric.

Gooseberry   Currant, gooseberry.

Grape   Grapes, raisins, sultanas, wine, (cream of tartar).

Grass   Wheat, spelt wheat, corn (maize), oats, barley, rye, rice, malt, millet, quinoa, bamboo shoots, sugar cane, sorghum, kamut.

Laurel   Avocado, cinnamon, bay leaves.

Lily   Onion, garlic, asparagus, chives, leeks.

Madder   Coffee.

Mallow   Okra, hibiscus.

Maple   Maple syrup.

Melon   Watermelon, cantaloupe and other melons, cucumber, zucchini, marrow, pumpkin, acorn squash and other squashes.

Mint   Apple mint, basil, bergamot, hyssop, lavender, lemon balm, marjoram, oregano, peppermint, rosemary, sage, spearmint, savory, thyme.

Mollusc   Abalone, snail, squid, clam, mussel, oyster, scallop, octopus.

Morning glory   Sweet potato.

Mulberry   Figs, mulberry, hops, breadfruit.

Mustard   Turnip, swede, radish, daikon, horseradish, Chinese leaves, watercress, mustard and cress, cabbage, cauliflower, broccoli, Brussels sprouts, kohlrabi, kale, mustard seed, rape seed.

Myrtle   Allspice, cloves, guava.

Nutmeg   Nutmeg, mace.

Olive   Black or green olives.

Orchid   Vanilla.

Palm   Coconut, date, date sugar, sago.

Papaya   Papaya.

Parsley   Carrots, parsnips, celery, celeriac, fennel, anise, parsley, caraway, lovage, chervil, coriander, cumin, dill.

Pea   Pea, sugar peas, mangetout, runner beans, French beans, broad beans, dried beans (*aduki beans, black beans, black-eyed beans, butter beans, cannellini beans, chickpeas, flageolet beans, haricot beans, lima beans, mung beans, dried peas, split green peas, split yellow peas, pinto beans, red kidney beans, soya beans*), lentils (*brown lentils, continental lentils, puy lentils, split red lentils*), alfalfa sprouts, liquorice, peanuts, fenugreek, red clover, senna, carob, Rooibosch tea.

Pedalium   Sesame seeds.

Pepper   Black and white pepper, peppercorn.

Pineapple   Pineapple.

Plum   Plum, damson, sloe, cherry, peach, apricot, nectarine, prune, almond.

Potato   Potato, tomato, aubergine (eggplant), peppers (capsicum), paprika, cayenne, chilli, tobacco.

Protea   Macadamia nuts.

Rabbit   Hare, rabbit.

Rose   Strawberry, raspberry, blackberry, loganberry, rosehip.

Saltwater fish   Tuna, mackerel, herring, eel, halibut, turbot, anchovy, sardine and pilchard, whitebait, sprats, sea bass, plaice, sole, cod, hake, haddock, sea bream, mullet.

Seaweed   Arame, nori, carrageen, wakeman, dulse, kelp, kombu, agar-agar.

Soapberry   Lychees.

Spurge   Cassava (tapioca).

Sterculia   Cocoa.

Subucaya   Brazil nut.

Swine   Pork, wild boar.

Tea   Tea, green leaf tea.

Walnut   Walnut, hickory nut, butternut, pecan.

Water chestnut   Water chestnut.

Yam   Yam.

Verbenum   Lemon verbena.

CHAPTER 3

The Preliminary Diet

The Preliminary Diet can include the following foods:

Cereals and flours   Brown rice, brown rice flour and rice bran and rice pasta; millet, millet flakes, flour and pasta; tapioca, tapioca flour; arrowroot, buckwheat, buckwheat flakes, flour and pasta; amaranth, sorghum; gram flour (chickpea); lima bean flour; lentil flour; sago and sago flour; sweet potato flour; chestnut flour; green banana flour (plantain); brazil nut flour; carob.

Meats   Lamb, lambs' liver and kidneys; rabbit; hare; venison; wild game birds.

Fish   Fresh tuna; sardines and pilchards; herrings; mackerel; mullet; turbot; halibut; sprats; whitebait, anchovy.

Drinks and sugars   Mineral water; plain herb teas like linden, peppermint, sage, camomile, lemon balm, rosehip, fennel, equisetum tea, African Rooibosch tea; honey; fruit sugar; rice syrup; date syrup; maple syrup.

Vegetables   The parsley food family (carrots, parsnips, celery, celeriac, fennel); the mustard family (turnip, swede, radish, daikon, Chinese leaves, watercress, mustard and cress, cabbage, cauliflower, broccoli, Brussels sprouts, horseradish, daikon, kohlrabi, kale); the beet family (spinach, beetroot, Swiss chard); seaweeds, okra; the aster family (lettuce, chicory, endive, globe and Jerusalem artichoke, dandelion, sunflower, salsify); the pea family (pea, sugar peas, mangetout, runner beans, French beans, broad beans, dried beans (*aduki beans, black beans, black-eyed beans, butter beans, cannellini beans, chickpeas, flageolet beans, haricot beans, lima beans, mung beans, dried peas, split green peas, split yellow peas, pinto beans, red kidney beans, but not soya beans*), lentils (*brown lentils, continental lentils, puy lentils, split red lentils*), alfalfa sprouts, fenugreek, red clover, senna, carob but not peanuts); the melon family (cucumber, pumpkin, zucchini, marrow, squash); plantain; sweet potatoes; yams; eddoes, dasheen; cassava; breadfruit, olives.

Fruit   Bananas; pineapple; kiwi fruit; the rose family (raspberry, blackberry, loganberry, rosehip); blueberry, cranberry; the plum family (almond, plum, sloe, cherry, peach, apricot, nectarine, prune); pears, loquat, quince; gooseberry, red, black and white currants; melon, watermelon, cantaloupe melon, other melons, acorn squash; figs; papaya; avocado pear; grapes, raisins, sultanas, currants; dates; elderberries, guava, lychees.

Nuts and seeds   Almonds; the walnut family (walnuts, hickory nuts, butternuts, pecan nuts); brazil nuts; hazelnuts; chestnuts; tiger nuts; macadamia nuts; coconut; pine nuts; sunflower seeds; pumpkin seeds; sesame seeds and tahini.

Herbs and spices   The parsley family (parsley, caraway, dill, anise, fennel seeds, celery seeds, cumin, chervil, coriander, chervil, lovage); the mint family (mint, basil, lemon balm, rosemary, sage, thyme, savory, marjoram, oregano); lemon verbena; lemon grass; the aster family (camomile, tarragon, yarrow); borage; bay leaf; juniper berries; the ginger family (turmeric, ginger, cardamon); the nutmeg family (nutmeg, mace); cinnamon; the myrtle family (clove, allspice); mustard seeds; fenugreek; liquorice, hibiscus.

Oils   Olive oil; sunflower seed oil; safflower oil; flax seed oil (linseed); sesame seed oil; walnut oil; almond oil.

Special foods

Amaranth is a gluten-free cereal, closely related to the buckwheat family. It contains all the essential amino acids and is rich in iron. It is available at some healthfood stores or by mail order.

Buckwheat is a gluten- and wheat-free cereal, available at most healthfood stores. It can be bought in seed form, as flakes and as a flour. It is rich in potassium, the amino acid lysine, and rutin which is good for improving circulation and strengthening blood capillaries.

Kelp is a natural seaweed, rich in minerals and trace elements, particularly iodine. It may be used as a substitute for salt. It is available dried in tablet or powder form.

Millet is a gluten-free cereal, rich in minerals, particularly silicon which is needed for healthy bones, teeth, nails and hair.

Quinoa is a cereal similar to millet. It contains all the eight amino acids and is a rich source of calcium and iron. The seed is coated with a bitter substance (saponins) which can easily be removed by soaking overnight and then rinsing thoroughly.

Sorghum is similar in composition to corn but lower in fat and higher in protein. It is available at some healthfood stores or through mail order.

Sweet potatoes, yams, cassava, eddoes and dasheen are all tropical tubers which are high in carbohydrates and can be used like potatoes. They are available in most large supermarkets or at West Indian food stores.

Tahini is a spread made from sesame seeds. It can be purchased in healthfood stores and some supermarkets. Sesame seeds are very rich in calcium.

Tapioca comes from the cassava root and is sold as pearls, flakes or as a flour. It can be bought in most supermarket stores. It consists almost entirely of starch with traces of calcium and other minerals. It can be used in puddings, and as a thickener in soups and sauces.

Tiger nuts are in fact tubers, not nuts, and are about the size of peanuts. They are cultivated in Spain and are available at some healthfood stores. They can be used for making 'nut' milks and for eating raw as a snack.

Guidelines

Vegetables can be washed in tap water and then rinsed in mineral water. Remember to clean your teeth with mineral water and check that your toothpaste does not contain sugar or any other substance you are trying to avoid.

It is safer to alternate fruits so that you do not eat the same fruit for more than two days in a row. Allow at least two days before eating the same fruit again. This rule applies also to herbs, herb teas and tea. Use powdered ginger and other spices very sparingly and use carob powder only in the third week. Also take care with fruit sugar, honey, date syrup, rice syrup and maple syrup. Use very little and alternate them if necessary. Some people who are allergic to pollen may react to honey. Try to choose honey from bees which are unlikely to have been fed on sugar throughout the winter months, such as honey from Mexico, Argentina and Australia. Cold-pressed, organic honey is ideal.

If you feel better after three weeks of the Preliminary Diet, you can then introduce more foods following the plan laid out in the Elimination Diet. Start at Day 9 with the introduction of tap water and then continue through until Day 28. You will find that some of the foods in subsequent days, such as avocado pear, will not need to be tested as you will already have included them in the Preliminary Diet. All such foods are marked with an asterisk so that you will be able to recognize them immediately. You can simply introduce these foods into your diet as shown without having to test them. If, however, you do not feel any better and you have checked that you are not reacting to any chemicals or fumes, go to the beginning of the Elimination Diet procedure and start at Day 1.

The following menus are only suggestions. You can use any of the recipes in the following pages, as well as those from Days 1 to 8 inclusive, in the Elimination Diet.

Suggested menus

MONDAY

Breakfast: Rice muesli (rice flakes, hazelnuts, raisins), with cashew nut milk.

Main meal: Grilled mackerel or turbot with gooseberry sauce, served with mashed yam and fresh salad.
Quinoa nut roast served with fresh salad.

Light meal: Country vegetable broth with rice bread.

TUESDAY

Breakfast: Millet and buckwheat muesli (millet and buckwheat flakes, chopped almonds, sultanas, dates) with almond milk.

Main meal: Game bird casserole, served with green vegetables.
Vegetable hash browns, served with fennel and bean sprout salad.

Light meal: Cream of cauliflower soup with almonds.

WEDNESDAY

Breakfast: Millet porridge with fresh banana.

Main meal: Lamb burgers served with sweet potatoes and green vegetables.
Quinoa and zucchini risotto.

Light meal: Fish soup.

THURSDAY

Breakfast: Quinoa porridge with hunza apricots.
Main meal: Braised venison with juniper, served with redcurrant sauce, broccoli and sweet potatoes.
Steamed vegetables with millet.
Light meal: Celery and zucchini soup.

FRIDAY

Breakfast: Rice porridge with fresh pears.
Main meal: Red mullet with seasoned rice stuffing, served with spinach.
Millet, lentil and brazil nut loaf, served with green vegetables or salad.
Light meal: Green split pea soup with broccoli.

SATURDAY

Breakfast: Rice and buckwheat porridge with fresh raspberries.
Main meal: Rabbit hot pot, served with fresh green vegetables.
Parsnip and walnut croquettes, served with raw salad or steamed vegetables.
Light meal: Celery and chestnut soup.

SUNDAY

Breakfast: Fresh melon with ginger.
Main meal: Wild duck with pineapple, served with sweet potatoes and cauliflower.
Apricot and almond pilaff with fresh salad.
Light meal: Cream of carrot and celeriac soup.

Recipes

To cook rice

225g (8oz; 1 cup) organic wholegrain rice
600ml (1¼ pints; 2¼ cups) mineral water
pinch of sea salt

Rinse the rice and place it in a saucepan with the salt. Pour over the water and bring to the boil. Turn the heat down, place the lid on the saucepan and simmer gently for 30 minutes until all the water has been absorbed. Do not rinse as this will wash away the nutrients. If there is too much water, strain and use the liquid in soup.

To cook pre-soaked rice, use the same water that was used for soaking, adding more to make up the quantity if necessary, and follow the above procedure. The cooking time should be reduced to approximately 15 minutes.

Rice porridge can be made using short-grain rice and twice as much water. Simmer gently for 40 to 50 minutes.

To cook millet, quinoa or amaranth

Follow the method for rice, reducing the amount of water from 2¼ cups to 2 cups (500ml; 1 pint).

To cook sorghum

225g (8oz; 1 cup) sorghum
1 litre (1¾ pints; 4 cups) mineral water

Cook as for rice, increasing the time to one hour.

To cook lentils

Place the lentils in a saucepan with sufficient boiling water to cover, and a pinch of salt. Cook gently until tender. The cooking time will vary according to how long the lentils have been sprouted. Sprouted lentils can be steamed.

Dairy substitutes, breads, jam and biscuits

Rice milk

50g (2oz; ¼ cup) organic short wholegrain rice
1 litre (1¾ pints; 4 cups) mineral water
1 tbsp safflower oil (optional)
1–2 tsp honey (optional)
1 vanilla pod (optional)

Wash the grains and place in a saucepan with the water. Add the vanilla pod if desired, then bring to the boil and simmer gently for 20 minutes to 1 hour. Cool slightly and then liquidize. Pour through a strainer and discard the pulp or save it to use in recipes. Add the honey, and more water if necessary. Add the safflower oil when completely cool and keep refrigerated.

Almond milk

125g (4oz; 1 cup) blanched almonds
1 litre (1¾ pints; 4 cups) mineral water
1–2 tsp honey
pinch of cinnamon

Blend the almonds and some of the water in a liquidizer for at least a minute until the mixture is very smooth. Add the honey, cinnamon and remaining water, strain and serve.

Walnut, pecan nut and brazil nut milks can all be made in the same way.

Almond or cashew nut cream

Follow the recipe for nut milk, reducing the water to 125ml (¼ pint; ½ cup). Other nuts can be used in the same way.

Sunflower and sesame seed milk

75g (3oz; ¾ cup) organic sunflower seeds
25g (1oz; ¼ cup) sesame seeds
½ litre (1 pint; 2 cups) mineral water
50g (2oz; ½ cup) organic dried dates

Rinse the seeds and liquidize with some of the water. When smooth, add the dates and the remaining water, blend again and serve. The fruit and seeds may be pre-soaked overnight.

Tiger nut milk

225g (8oz; 1⅓ cups) tiger nuts, washed and soaked overnight
1 litre (1¾ pints; 4 cups) mineral water

Rinse the tiger nuts. Liquidize with the water and strain off the pulp. Use the milk to pour over cereal and keep or freeze the pulp to use in recipes.

Nut and seed butters

Use any type of raw nut or seed. (Pre-soaking overnight will make them sweeter and more digestible.)

Rinse off any water and grind in a liquidizer by dropping seeds or nuts a few at a time onto the rotating blades, through the opening in the lid of the liquidizer.

Rice bread

125g (4oz; 1 cup) rice flakes
1 cup mineral water
125g (4oz; 1 cup) pea or lentil flour
125g (4oz; 1 cup) almonds or brazil nuts, ground
125g (4oz; 1 cup) kohlrabi, grated
2 tbsp sesame seed oil or olive oil
1 tbsp tapioca flour or arrowroot
1 tsp cream of tartar
½ tsp bicarbonate of soda
½ tsp sea salt

Preheat the oven to 150°C (300°F), Gas Mark 2.

Pour the water onto the rice flakes and leave to soak for 5 minutes, to soften them. Mix all the ingredients together and bake in a lined 2lb loaf tin for 1 hour until firm.

Rice and sago bread

125g (4oz; 1 cup) sago pearls
125g (4oz; 1 cup) rice flour
50g (2oz; ½ cup) lentil flour
1½ cups mineral water
1 tsp cream of tartar
½ tsp bicarbonate of soda

Preheat the oven to 150°C (300°F), Gas Mark 2.

Pour the water onto the sago and leave to soak for 30 minutes to soften. Mix with the remaining ingredients and bake in a lined 1lb loaf tin for 45 minutes.

Hedgerow jam

675g (1½lb; 6 cups) blackberries
225g (8oz; 2 cups) elderberries
225g (8oz; 2 cups) rosehips
125g (4oz; 1 cup) sloes
250ml (½ pint; 1 cup) pear juice
½ litre (1 pint; 2 cups) mineral water
2 tbsp tapioca flour or arrowroot

Wash the fruit thoroughly and then stew in the water until

soft. Pour through a sieve and discard the pulp. Stir in the pear juice to sweeten, and thicken with arrowroot or tapioca flour. Keep refrigerated or freeze in small portions.

Carob and walnut brownies

125g (4oz; 1 cup) brown rice flour
50g (2oz; ½ cup) carob powder
50g (2oz; ½ cup) green banana flour
125g (4oz; 1 cup) dates, chopped
125g (4oz; 1 cup) sultanas
125g (4oz; 1 cup) walnuts, roughly chopped
125ml (4 floz; ½ cup) olive oil or sesame seed oil
250ml (½ pint; 1 cup) mineral water
1 tsp cinnamon

Preheat the oven to 160°C (310°F), Gas Mark 3.

Soften the dates in a little hot water and then mix all the ingredients together. Turn into a flat baking tin 27cm (11in) x 18cm (7in) and bake for 45 minutes. Allow to cool in the tin before cutting into squares.

Stocks and soups

Lamb stock

Use raw bones from organically reared mutton or lamb, chopped into 5cm (2in) pieces. Wash the bones and place them in a large heavy saucepan or pressure cooker.

Cover with cold mineral water and a pinch of sea salt and bring to the boil. Simmer for 3 hours or for 1½ hours in a pressure cooker.

Strain the stock and allow to cool. Skim off the fat before use. The stock may be frozen in an ice cube tray, or kept in a refrigerator for up to two days.

Game stock may be made in a similar way, but cooking time should be reduced to 2 hours, or 1 hour in a pressure cooker.

Fish stock

Wash the trimmings and break up the bones. Cover with cold mineral water, add a little sea salt and bring to simmering point. Cook gently for no longer than 30 minutes to avoid bitterness. The stock may be frozen in an ice cube tray.

Vegetable stock (potassium broth)

Use vegetables, seaweeds and trimmings, but note that too many mustard family greens or too much spinach may spoil the flavour. Simmer gently with plenty of mineral water and with the lid on the saucepan for 1½ to 2 hours. The nutrients will leach into the stock which can then be strained off and the fibre remains discarded. If you are freezing the stock, take great care to label it with all the ingredients, as you will need to know the exact contents when checking your allergies.

Cream of cauliflower soup with almonds

1 small cauliflower
1 small sweet potato, peeled and roughly chopped
3 sticks celery
1 litre (1¾ pints; 4 cups) mineral water or stock
125g (4oz; 1 cup) ground almonds
sea salt

Bring the water or stock to the boil. Add the cauliflower, sweet potato and celery, and a pinch of salt. Cook for 5 to 7 minutes until the vegetables are tender.

Allow to cool slightly, then take out a few cauliflower florets and put them to one side. Add the ground almonds to the soup and liquidize until smooth. Return the soup to the pan. Add the cauliflower florets and reheat gently.

Celery and zucchini soup

6 sticks celery, diced
2 zucchini, cut lengthways and sliced
1 small sweet potato or yam, diced
1 litre (1¾ pints; 4 cups) stock or mineral water
sea salt or kelp
fresh coriander leaves, chopped

Bring the stock or water to the boil and add the vegetables. Cover and cook for 10 minutes until the vegetables are tender.

Ladle out half the vegetables and liquidize then to a purée. Return them to the pan, reheat and serve with a garnishing of coriander or another herb chosen from the list on page 20.

Green split pea soup with broccoli

125g (4oz; ⅔ cup) green split peas
450g (1lb; 4 cups) broccoli, chopped
125g (4oz; 1 cup) broccoli florets
1 litre (1¾ pints; 4 cups) stock and/or mineral water
2 bay leaves
½ tsp dried marjoram
½ tsp ground lemon grass
1 tsp sea salt

Pre-soak the split peas in hot water for 1 to 2 hours (like yellow split peas, these will not sprout). Place in a pan with the stock or mineral water, bay leaves, herbs and seasoning and cook for about 30 minutes until tender.

Add the broccoli and any remaining stock and cook for a further 10 minutes. Remove the bay leaves and leave the soup to cool slightly. Liquidize until smooth and return to the pan to reheat.

Meanwhile, steam the broccoli florets in a little water until tender but still green and add to the soup just before serving.

Celery and chestnut soup

125g (4oz; 1 cup) dried chestnuts, soaked overnight
1 bunch of celery, roughly sliced
1 litre (1¾ pints; 4 cups) stock or mineral water
1 bay leaf
freshly chopped parsley
sea salt

Cook the chestnuts in half the water for 1 hour. Meanwhile steam the celery or gently sauté in olive oil, reserving one or two finely diced sticks for garnishing. Cool slightly and liquidize to a purée with the drained chestnuts. Add the remaining stock or water and seasoning. Reheat and serve garnished with the diced celery and parsley.

Fish soup

2 mackerel
1 turnip
125g (4oz; 1 cup) cauliflower florets
1 tsp ground mustard seeds
1 litre (1¾ pints; 4 cups) fish stock or mineral water
1 tsp ground lemon grass
sea salt or kelp

Remove the heads, fins and tails from the fish and discard or use to make fish stock. Clean the fish throroughly, then poach gently in a pan with just enough mineral water to cover. Add the salt and mustard. Cook for about 7 minutes.

Remove the fish from the pan and remove the skins and backbones. Divide the flesh into pieces. Chop the vegetables and cook in the fish stock until tender. Add the pieces of fish and sprinkle with ground lemon grass.

Country vegetable broth

2 large carrots, diced
1 small parsnip, diced
3 sticks celery, diced
1 litre (1¾ pints; 4 cups) stock or mineral water
50g (2oz; ¼ cup) short-grain brown rice, pre-soaked overnight

25g (1oz; ¼ cup) green lentils, pre-soaked until just sprouting
2 bay leaves
2 tbsp chopped parsley
sea salt

Bring the stock or mineral water to the boil and add the
ingredients. Bring to the boil again and simmer for 20
minutes, stirring occasionally.

Remove the bay leaves and serve garnished with chopped
parsley.

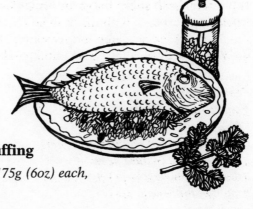

Main meals

Red mullet with seasoned rice stuffing

4 red mullet, about 175g (6oz) each,
cleaned and scaled
sea salt

FOR THE STUFFING:
175g (6oz; 1 cup) cooked long-grain rice
50g (2oz; ½ cup) pine nuts
50g (2oz; ½ cup) sultanas
50g (2oz; ½ cup) chopped olives (not in vinegar)
1 tsp ground lemon grass
1 tsp coriander leaves
sea salt

Preheat the oven to 180°C (350°F), Gas Mark 4.

Mix together the ingredients for the stuffing. Fill the cavity
of each fish with the stuffing and secure with a skewer. Place
the fish on a well-oiled baking tray, sprinkle with sea salt, and
bake for 30 to 35 minutes.

Grilled sardines with herbs

900g (2lb) fresh sardines (about 12)
2 tbsp chopped mixed herbs (lemon balm, basil or mint)
sea salt

Remove the heads from the sardines, slit open the undersides and remove the entrails. Wash the sardines and dry them thoroughly.

Place the sardines on an oiled grill tray, sprinkle with 1 tablespoon of fresh herbs and a little sea salt. Grill for 2 to 3 minutes on both sides. Serve immediately, garnished with the remaining herbs.

Rabbit hot pot

1 whole rabbit or 4 rabbit portions
2 carrots, sliced
2 sticks celery, sliced
1 or 2 sweet potatoes, diced
1 turnip, diced
½ litre (1 pint; 2 cups) mineral water
1 tbsp fresh tarragon
½ tsp mustard seeds
1 tbsp sago flour
sea salt

Place the rabbit in a pan of boiling mineral water. Bring the water back to the boil, then add the vegetables and seasoning. Cook gently for 45 minutes to 1 hour until the rabbit is tender. Mix the sago flour with a little cold mineral water and use it to thicken the cooking juices.

Lamb burgers

175g (6oz; 1½ cups) lean lamb
50g (2oz; ½ cup) lambs' liver
125g (4oz; 1 cup) chestnut flour
freshly chopped parsley
sea salt

Mince the lamb and the liver. Mix together with the chestnut flour and seasoning and shape into four burgers about 2.5cm

(1in) thick, or use a burger press. Grill for 4 to 5 minutes on each side.

Devilled lambs' kidneys

4 lambs' kidneys
2 tbsp gram flour (chickpea flour)
250ml (½ pint; 1 cup) lamb stock
1 tsp ground mustard seeds
sea salt (optional)

Wash the kidneys in cold water. Dry and remove the cores. Cut into thin slices and roll each slice in the gram flour, sprinkle with mustard, and a little sea salt if liked.

Heat the stock in a pan, add the kidneys and cook gently for 4 or 5 minutes.

Braised venison with juniper

4 venison steaks
2 sticks celery, sliced
2 carrots, diced
8 juniper berries
½ litre (1 pint; 2 cups) stock or mineral water
1 tbsp sago or tapioca flour
olive oil
sea salt
chopped parsley

Preheat the oven to 160°C (310°F), Gas Mark 3.

Grill the steaks on both sides to seal, then place them in an ovenproof casserole dish. Add the vegetables, juniper berries and sea salt, and cover with the stock. Cook for one hour until the meat is tender. Mix the sago flour with a little cold mineral water and add to the juices to thicken the sauce.

Garnish with chopped parsley and serve with redcurrant sauce (see page 36).

Redcurrant sauce

225g (8oz; 2 cups) redcurrants
250ml (½ pint; 1 cup) mineral water
1 tbsp fruit sugar, honey or maple syrup
2 tsp sago or tapioca flour

Place the redcurrants in a saucepan with the water. Bring to
the boil and simmer until cooked. Add the sweetener and
thicken with the sago or tapioca flour, mixed with a little cold
mineral water.

Wild duck with pineapple

900g (2lb) oven-ready wild duck
1 carrot, cut into strips
1 celery stalk, sliced
1 bay leaf
1 sprig thyme
250ml (½ pint; 1 cup) stock or mineral water
1 small pineapple
sea salt

Preheat the oven to 190°C (375°F), Gas Mark 5.

Place the duck in an ovenproof casserole dish and add the
vegetables, stock or water, bay leaf, thyme and salt and cook
for 1½ hours, reducing the oven temperature to 160°C (310°F),
Gas Mark 3 after the first 15 minutes. Baste the duck from
time to time and add more water if necessary. When cooked,
lift the duck onto a serving dish and keep it warm.

Remove the skin from the pineapple, and cut the flesh into
slices 1cm (½in) thick. Cook in the remaining juice, simmering
for approximately 2 minutes. Remove the bay leaf and thyme.

Garnish the duck with pineapple and pour over the juice
before serving.

Salads and vegetarian meals

Millet, lentil and brazil nut loaf

125g (4oz; ½ cup) millet
125g (4oz; ⅔ cup) green lentils, sprouted
1 cup vegetable stock or mineral water
1 tbsp tapioca flour
125g (4oz; 1 cup) brazil nuts, roughly chopped
2 sticks celery, diced
1 tbsp fresh sage
sea salt

Preheat the oven to 160°C (310°F), Gas Mark 3.

Cook the millet and lentils in the stock or mineral water and mix with the rest of the ingredients. Oil a 1lb loaf tin or deep pie dish and press the mixture well in.

Bake for 45 minutes or until the top of the loaf is brown and firm to the touch. Serve hot or cold.

Fennel and bean sprout salad

1 large fennel, thinly sliced
225g (8oz; 2 cups) bean sprouts
½ cucumber, sliced
1 zucchini, diced
125g (4oz; 1 cup) seedless green grapes
1 nectarine, cut into segments
4 Chinese leaves, shredded

Arrange the ingredients on a bed of shredded Chinese leaves.

Quinoa and zucchini risotto

225g (8oz; 1 cup) quinoa
450g (1lb; 4 cups) zucchini, sliced
½ litre (1 pint; 2 cups) mineral water
1 tbsp cold-pressed olive oil
sea salt
1 tsp dried basil

Rinse the quinoa in a strainer and put in a saucepan with a
pinch of sea salt. Cover with mineral water and bring to the
boil. Simmer for 15 minutes and then add the sliced zucchini.
Cook for a further 5 minutes until all the mineral water has
been absorbed. Add the olive oil just before serving and
garnish with basil.

Arame with sesame seeds

125g (4oz; 2 cups) dried and shredded arame
1 carrot, cut into matchsticks
50g (2oz; ½ cup) sesame seeds

Rinse the arame seaweed and place it in a pan with enough
cold mineral water to cover. Leave it to soak for 10 minutes.
Add the carrot and bring to the boil and simmer for 30
minutes until all the water has been absorbed. Turn into a
serving dish.

Sprinkle the sesame seeds over the arame.

Quinoa nut roast

(Serves 6-8)
225g (8oz; 1 cup) quinoa, cooked
125g (4oz; 1 cup) carrots, grated
125g (4oz; 1 cup) zucchini, grated
2 sticks celery, chopped
125g (4oz; 1 cup) ground almonds
50g (2oz; ½ cup) whole almonds, chopped
125g (4oz; 1 cup) sunflower seeds
4 tbsp olive oil
125ml (¼ pint; ½ cup) vegetable stock or mineral water

2 tbsp sago flour
fresh sage or tarragon, chopped or 1 tsp dried
sea salt

Preheat the oven to 160°C (310°F), Gas Mark 3.

Line a 2lb loaf tin with greaseproof paper. Mix all the ingredients together and turn into the tins. Bake for 1 hour.

Use any of the soups on pages 30 to 53 as a sauce and serve hot. The nut roast can also be eaten cold and is ideal for picnics.

CHAPTER 4
The Elimination Diet Plan

This section provides a 28-day plan for detecting your food intolerances.

Days 1 to 4

Eat any of the following: **pears**, **rice** and **lamb** or **lentils**, seasoned with sea salt. Drink only mineral water for the first two days, but on Days 3 and 4 you can also have equisetum (horsetail) and linden leaf tea.

Suggested menu

On rising, drink two glasses of hot water.

8am: One or two fresh pears.

10am: Grilled lamb or a serving of lentils and rice.

1pm: Lamb with rice or lentils with rice.

4pm: Fresh pear.

6pm: Rice porridge with cooked pears.

9pm: Fresh pear.

If you suffer from arthritis, you may find that red meat is too acidic for you, in which case you may want to avoid lamb altogether and substitute lentils or vegetables from the mustard family such as broccoli, cauliflower, cabbage, watercress or Chinese leaves.

It is very important to exclude everything else from your diet. A small drink of tea or coffee could alter the whole experiment and you would need to start again. Smoking could also affect your diet's results. This may seem extreme, but it is worth persevering. The diet is for a relatively short amount of time and it can bring a lifetime's benefit.

During the first four days you are likely to feel unwell due to withdrawal symptoms, but by the fifth day you should feel better and will be able to start the re-introduction of foods. Foods are re-introduced according to their food family. When you test the foods, you will be able to tell whether or not you are allergic or intolerant to them. If you react to any foods you should avoid them from then on. The recipes have been designed to make this as easy as possible for you. If you do not react, you can then simply introduce them into your diet as the plan shows you. You may notice that some foods will not be introduced into the diet immediately after testing. This is simply a precaution in case you react more slowly to them as some people do. The majority of foods, though, will produce immediately recognizable symptoms.

Symptoms might well vary from food to food. Some foods will produce more severe reactions; others will be more delayed. The types of symptoms can also differ enormously. Sometimes, for example, you may experience panic attacks, other times just a faint headache. This is where the pulse test is invaluable (see page 10). Do not forget to use this and then to record all reactions in your food diary (see page 9).

If you can, try to test the foods in as many different ways

as possible – raw, lightly cooked and cooked slowly for a longer time – as this may make a difference to whether or not you react. The recipes and the menus have been designed to help you to do this. Do not worry, though, if you cannot test all the members of each food family. There are, of course, exceptions to the rule, but normally if you react to one member of a family, you will do so to all the others. Those that are the normal exceptions have been introduced separately into the 28-day plan.

For those with multiple food intolerances, it may be that you will need to slow the diet down a little. For some people, just introducing one new food or food family at a time will be sufficient. Remember that this is a diet about getting well, not about racing to the end. If you are unsure about a reaction, you can leave the food family out and test again in four days' time.

You may find that you are trying out new foods that you have not eaten before. This is a good idea, not only because it offers you delicious new foods, but it will also mean that your diet will not be as limited as it might have been if you have to start avoiding certain foods. So try the quails' eggs, the venison and the tiger nuts, for example. They are delicious and a way of ensuring that you do not feel you are depriving yourself.

Day 5

Introduce and test the following: **mustard family** (turnip, swede, radish, daikon, watercress, mustard and cress, Chinese leaves, cabbage, cauliflower, broccoli, Brussels sprouts, kohlrabi, kale, mustard seeds); **kiwi fruit; flax seed oil** (linseed oil). Flax seed oil may be sprinkled on salads or added to mashed vegetables but do not use it for cooking. Lamb dripping can be saved for this purpose.

Suggested menu

Breakfast: Fresh pears with rice porridge.
Vegetable hash browns.

Main meal: Grilled lamb with green vegetables and mashed swede.
Rice and lentils with green vegetables and mashed swede.

Light meal: Turnip and watercress soup.
Steamed vegetables with rice.

Raw salad: Sliced Chinese leaves, watercress, mustard and cress, radishes or grated daikon, dressed with safflower oil.

Fruit: Pears, kiwi fruit.

Drinks: Mineral water, linden leaf tea, rice milk (see page 26).

Vegetable hash browns

225g (8oz; 2 cups) turnip or swede, cooked and mashed
125g (4oz; 1 cup) finely sliced and chopped white cabbage
125g (4oz; 1 cup) brown rice flour
sea salt

Preheat the oven to 160°C (310°F), Gas Mark 3.

Mix all the ingredients together and shape into cakes. Place on a baking tray and cook for 20 minutes.

The hash browns may be made up in larger quantities for freezing.

Turnip and watercress soup

450g (1lb; 4 cups) turnips, peeled and roughly chopped
1 litre (1¾ pints; 4 cups) lamb stock and/or mineral water
1 bunch watercress
sea salt

Wash the watercress thoroughly and separate the stalks from the leaves.

Bring the stock or water to the boil and add the turnips. Simmer until tender. Liquidize with the watercress stalks and return to the pan. Add the watercress leaves and cook for a further minute.

Steamed vegetables

225g (8oz; 2 cups) broccoli florets
225g (8oz; 2 cups) swede, cut into julienne strips
225g (8oz; 2 cups) kohlrabi, diced
125g (4oz; 1 cup) turnip, diced
75g (3oz; ¾ cup) radishes, sliced
75g (3oz; ¾ cup) cabbage, shredded
sea salt
flax seed oil (optional)

Using a steamer or just a small amount of water, cook the vegetables with the sea salt. Start with the root vegetables (swede, kohlrabi, turnip and radish) then add the broccoli florets and finish with the cabbage. The vegetables may be served with a sprinkling of flax seed oil.

Day 6

You now need to come off rice, pears, lentils and lamb in order to test them on Day 9.

Soak the tiger nuts for Day 7 overnight.

You can now introduce and test the following: **quinoa; sweet potato, dasheen** and **eddoe; fruit sugar; olive oil; saltwater fish** (mackerel, sardine, herring, fresh tuna, anchovy, halibut, turbot, red or grey mullet, whitebait); **mallow family** (okra, hibiscus); **melon family** (watermelon, cantaloupe and other melons, cucumber, zucchini, marrow, pumpkin, acorn squash and other squashes); **gooseberry family** (gooseberry, red, white and blackcurrants); **elderberries**; **mint family** (fresh peppermint tea, sage, basil, lemon balm, thyme, rosemary, marjoram, oregano).

Suggested menu

Breakfast: Melon.
Quinoa porridge with stewed gooseberries or kiwi fruit.

Main meal: Grilled sardines (see page 34) with baked sweet potato and cucumber salad.
Grilled mackerel with gooseberry sauce, mashed sweet potato, zucchini or watercress and cucumber salad.
Quinoa and zucchini risotto with sweet potato chips and raw salad.

Light meal: Fish soup (see page 32)
Sweet potato and seafood bakes.
Zucchini and sweet potato bakes.

Raw salad: Cucumbers, suitable vegetables from the mustard family and okra.

Fruit: Melon, stewed or raw blackcurrants or gooseberries.

Drinks: Mineral water, herb tea made from peppermint, lemon balm, sage, thyme, rosemary or hibiscus.

Quinoa porridge

(Serves 1)
75g (3oz; ½ cup) quinoa (preferably soaked overnight)
450ml (¾ pint; 1¼ cups) mineral water

Put the quinoa in a pan with the water and bring to the boil.
Simmer for 20 to 30 minutes until well cooked.

Grilled mackerel with gooseberry sauce

4 mackerel
sea salt

FOR THE SAUCE:
450g (1lb; 4 cups) gooseberries
2 tbsp mineral water
1 tbsp fruit sugar

Thoroughly wash and dry the mackerel and place them on an
oiled grill tray. Score deep gashes across each fish to allow the
heat to penetrate. Season with salt and grill for 8 to 10
minutes until cooked. There should be no need to turn.

To prepare the sauce, top and tail the gooseberries and
cook them with the water until soft. Liquidize or rub through
a sieve and return to the pan. Add the fruit sugar and serve
hot with the mackerel.

Gooseberry sauce is also good with other oily fish such as
herrings, sardines, turbot or halibut.

Sweet potato and seafood bakes

225g (8oz; 2 cups) tuna fish, cooked
225g (8oz; 2 cups) sweet potato, cooked and mashed
sea salt
basil, fresh or dried
quinoa flour

Preheat the oven to 160°C (310°F), Gas Mark 3.
Mix together the sweet potato, tuna fish, basil and salt. Make
into cakes and roll each one in flour. Bake for 20 minutes,
turning once.

For larger quantities, the mixture may be formed into a roll
on a lightly floured board and cut into slices before shaping
and flouring. The uncooked cakes can be frozen.

Zucchini bakes may be made in a similar way, substituting grated zucchini for tuna fish.

Sweet potatoes may be cooked in the same way as potatoes – boiled, mashed or baked, but do not fry. A large sweet potato weighing 450g (1lb; 4 cups) will take 1 hour to cook at 160°C (310°F), Gas Mark 3. Do not overcook.

Day 7

Prepare and soak lentils and beans today that you wish to use on Day 9.

Introduce and test the following: **millet, cassava** (tapioca); **maple syrup; buckwheat family** (buckwheat, rhubarb, sorrel, amaranth); **wild game bird** (pigeon, wild duck, partridge, grouse, pheasant); **walnut family** (walnuts, pecan nuts, hickory nut, butternut, walnut oil); **tiger nuts; parsley family** (carrots, parsnips, celery, celeriac, fennel, anise, parsley, caraway, dill, cumin, coriander, chervil, lovage); **banana family** (banana, plantain, arrowroot); **pineapple; papaya.** Nuts and seeds can be tested on their own, before adding to recipes.

Suggested menu

Breakfast: Diced pineapple and banana fruit salad.
Millet porridge.
Millet and buckwheat muesli with pecan nuts, banana and tiger nut milk.

Main meal: Game bird casserole with broccoli, Brussels sprouts or other green vegetables.
Parsnip and walnut croquettes served with carrots and green vegetables.

Light meal: Cream of carrot and celeriac soup.
Celery, walnut and fennel salad with buckwheat pasta.
Grated carrot, celery and nut salad with millet.

Puddings: Baked bananas with chopped pecan nuts and maple syrup.

Drinks: Mineral water, fennel tea.

Millet and millet porridge can be cooked in the same way as quinoa or you can use millet flakes. Buckwheat and millet flakes may be used to make up the muesli.

Game bird casserole

A brace of grouse, partridge or 3 pigeons
3 or 4 carrots
1 parsnip
2 sticks of celery, sliced
½ litre (1 pint; 2 cups) mineral water
2 tsp chopped parsley
sea salt
2 tsp tapioca flour

Preheat the oven to 190°C (375°F), Gas Mark 5.

Place the game birds in an ovenproof casserole dish. Add the vegetables, left whole or cut where necessary, parsley and salt and pour in the boiling water.

Cook for 1½ hours, reducing the temperature of the oven to 160°C (310°F), Gas Mark 3 after the first 20 minutes.

Place the game birds and the vegetables on a hot serving dish. Skim off any fat and use the cooking juices to make a gravy, using a little tapioca flour mixed with some cold water to thicken. Carve the game birds and divide the vegetables as necessary to serve.

Parsnip and walnut croquettes

225g (8oz; 2 cups) cooked parsnips
225g (8oz; 2 cups) cooked sweet potato or eddoe
2 sticks celery, finely diced
125g (4oz; 1 cup) walnuts, chopped
1 tsp tapioca flour
1 tbsp fresh coriander, chopped
sea salt
1 tbsp millet flour

Preheat the oven to 160°C (310°F), Gas Mark 3.

Mash the parsnips and sweet potato or eddoe and mix the ingredients together and form into eight croquettes. Roll in millet flour and place on baking tray and bake for 35 minutes.

Some of the carrot and celeriac soup (see below), made thicker with less water, may be used as a sauce.

Cream of carrot and celeriac soup

275g (10oz; 2½ cups) carrots, chopped
275g (10oz; 2½ cups) celeriac, chopped
1 litre (1¾ pints; 4 cups) mineral water, game stock or parsley
* family stock*
2 tbsp parsley or coriander leaves, chopped
sea salt

Cook the vegetables in some of the stock or water until tender.
  Liquidize the vegetables until smooth and creamy. Return to the pan, add the remaining liquid and salt and reheat. Cook for a further two minutes and serve with a garnishing of chopped parsley or coriander leaves.

Day 8

You can now test and introduce the following foods into your diet: **yam**; **sago**; **sorghum**; **rabbit** and **hare**; **aster family** (lettuce, chicory, endive, salsify, globe and Jerusalem artichoke, dandelion, sunflower seeds, tarragon, camomile, yarrow); **plum family** (plum, sloe, cherry, peach, apricot, nectarine, prune, almond); **sunflower**, **safflower** and **almond oils**; **camomile tea**; **honey**.

Suggested menu

Breakfast: Fresh peaches and cherries.
Quinoa or sorghum porridge with cooked hunza or unsulphured apricots and almonds.
Main meal: Rabbit with prunes, served with mashed yam and lettuce salad.
'Almond and apricot pilaff with lettuce salad.
Light meal: Yam and chicory soup.
Boiled yam with lettuce and chicory salad.

Rabbit with prunes

4 rabbit portions
½ litre (1 pint; 2 cups) boiling water and prune juice
225g (8oz; 2 cups) cooked prunes and juice
2 tsp fresh tarragon, chopped
2 tsp sago flour
sea salt

Place the rabbit portions in a heavy-based saucepan and cover with the boiling water and prune juice. Add some salt, tarragon and any remaining prune juice. Cover with a lid and cook over a gentle heat for 20 minutes.

Lift out the rabbit portions and place them on a serving dish and keep warm.

Mix the sago flour with some cold water and stir into the cooking juices to make a sauce. Pour the sauce over the rabbit and arrange the prunes around.

This dish could be served on a bed of quinoa with a lettuce salad.

Apricot and almond pilaff

2 cups sorghum or quinoa
8 cups mineral water (sorghum) or 4 cups mineral water (quinoa)
175g (6oz; 1½ cups) fresh apricots, cut into quarters
125g (4oz; 1 cup) almonds
25g (1oz; ¼ cup) sunflower seeds

1 tsp fresh tarragon, chopped
2 tbsp sunflower oil
sea salt

Rinse the sorghum or quinoa and place in a saucepan with
the water and a pinch of salt. Bring to the boil and simmer for
1 hour (30 minutes for quinoa) until soft, adding the apricots
during the last 5 minutes of cooking time. Cut the almonds in
half lengthways and add them to the sorghum, together with
the tarragon. Serve garnished with the sunflower seeds and
pour over the sunflower oil.

Yam and chicory soup

225g (8oz; 2 cups) yam, peeled and chopped
½ litre (1 pint; 2 cups) mineral water or stock
2 heads of chicory, chopped
1 tbsp fresh tarragon, chopped
sea salt

Bring the water or stock to the boil. Add the yam and a pinch
of salt. Bring to the boil again and simmer until tender.

Liquidize the yam and return it to the pan. Add the chicory
and cook for 1 minute. Sprinkle with tarragon and serve.

Day 9

Test rice and re-introduce it on Day 11 if no adverse reactions have been experienced.

Introduce and test the following (*except foods already tested): ***pears, *quince, *loquat** and ***lychees; *lamb; *pea family** (pea, sugar peas, mangetout, runner beans, French beans, broad beans, dried beans (aduki beans, black beans, black-eyed beans, butter beans, cannellini beans, chickpeas, flageolet beans, haricot beans, lima beans, mung beans, dried peas, split green peas, split yellow peas, pinto beans, red kidney beans), lentils (brown lentils, continental lentils, puy lentils, split red lentils), **alfalfa sprouts, liquorice, fenugreek, red clover, senna, carob** (but test soya on Day 13 and peanuts on Day 25); ***brazil nuts; *macadamia nuts; *lemon verbena tea** and ***fenugreek tea**. Test **tap water** at the end of the day; if you experience no reaction you may start using filtered tap water instead of mineral water.

Suggested menu

Breakfast: Pears.
Millet and buckwheat flakes with lychees or kiwi fruit.
Main meal: Grilled lamb with peas or green beans and sweet potato.
Vegetable stir-fry served with millet.
Light meal: Lentil soup with rice cakes.
Brazil nut and bean burgers with green salad, boiled rice for testing.

Vegetable stir-fry

125g (4oz; 1 cup) swede, diced
125g (4oz; 1 cup) French beans, cut into half lengths
75g (3oz; ¾ cup) kale or green leafy cabbage, shredded
225g (8oz; 2 cups) bean sprouts
2–3 tbsp safflower oil

Pour a little water into the bottom of a wok or a heavy-based saucepan, and cook the vegetables quickly, starting with the root vegetable (swede) and then add the French beans, cabbage and bean sprouts. Spoon on the safflower oil and serve.

Lentil soup

125g (4oz; 1 cup) brown lentils, pre-soaked
2 large carrots
1 parsnip
2 sticks celery
1 litre (1¾ pints; 4 cups) water or stock
1 tsp ground cumin
1 tbsp coriander leaves, chopped
sea salt

Bring the water or stock to the boil. Add the lentils, roughly chopped vegetables, ground cumin and salt. Simmer gently until the vegetables are tender.

Liquidize and return to the pan to reheat.

Serve with a sprinkling of fresh coriander leaves.

Brazil nut and bean burgers

225g (8oz; 1⅓ cups) black-eyed beans, sprouted and cooked
125g (4oz; 1 cup) brazil nuts, soaked and chopped
125g (4oz; 1 cup) buckwheat flakes
2 tbsp safflower oil
1 tsp dried sage
sea salt
1 tsp millet flour

Preheat the oven to 160°C (310°F), Gas Mark 3.

Mix all the ingredients together, adding a little water to bind if necessary, and mould into burgers or use a burger press. Roll in millet flour and bake for 20 minutes.

Day 10

Test barley at the end of the day and introduce on Day 12 if
no adverse reaction has been experienced. Test beet sugar.
Introduce and test the following (*except foods already
tested): *venison; saltwater fish (cod, haddock, hake, plaice,
sole, sea bream, whiting); *beet family (spinach, Swiss chard,
beetroot, beet sugar); rose family (strawberry, *raspberry,
*blackberry, *loganberry, *rosehip); *conifer family (pine
nuts, juniper berries); *cashew family (cashew nuts, pistachio
nuts, mango); *mulberry family (figs, hops, mulberries,
breadfruit); *pumpkin seeds; *olives; *lemon grass tea;
*raspberry leaf tea.

Suggested menu

Breakfast: Compote of fresh strawberries and raspberries
mixed with cooked blackberries.
Quinoa porridge.

Main meal: Braised venison with juniper (page 35) served
with redcurrant sauce, sautéed sweet potatoes
and spinach.
Rolled plaice with spinach, served with carrots.
Butternut squash with pine nuts, served with
sweet potatoes.

Light meal: Swiss chard and celery soup with barley scone
bread.
Millet and cashew nut risotto, served with melon,
strawberry and cucumber salad.

Rolled plaice with spinach

4 fillets of plaice
675g (1½lb; 6 cups) spinach
50g (2oz; ½ cup) maize or millet flour
50g (2oz; ½ cup) ground cashew nuts
sea salt
sprigs of parsley

Preheat the oven to 160°C (310°F), Gas Mark 3.

Thoroughly wash the spinach, and steam it in its own moisture until tender. Mash it with a fork and place in a well-oiled casserole dish.

Cut the plaice fillets in two lengthways and roll up each half, securing it with a cocktail stick. Arrange them on top of the spinach and sprinkle with a mixture of millet flour, ground cashew nuts and sea salt. Cover and cook for 30 minutes. Serve garnished with parsley.

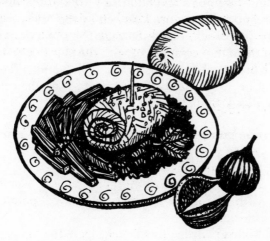

Butternut squash with pine nuts

675g (1½lb; 6 cups) butternut squash, winter squash or marrow
125g (4oz; 1 cup) pine nuts
1 tsp ground cumin or seeds
1 tsp ground lemon grass
sea salt
sprigs of fresh mint

Peel the squash and cut it in half lengthways, then cut it into crosswise slices. Discard the seeds.

Steam or cook the squash with a little boiling water, sprinkling in the salt, cumin and lemon grass. Cook for 4 to 5 minutes until just tender. Arrange the pieces in overlapping layers in a large shallow dish. Sprinkle over the pine nuts and garnish with mint. Serve hot or cold.

Swiss chard and celery soup

350g (12oz; 3 cups) Swiss chard or spinach
4 sticks celery
125g (4oz; 1 cup) sweet potato or yam, diced
1 litre (1¾ pints; 4 cups) stock or water
2 sprigs fresh thyme (or ½ tsp dried)
sea salt

Reserve a celery stick and a leaf of Swiss chard. Roughly chop the remaining vegetables and boil in a little water, starting with the sweet potato or yam, followed by the celery and Swiss chard or spinach. Blend the vegetables in a liquidizer, then return them to the saucepan with the stock or water and bring to the boil. Season with salt and thyme and add the reserved leaf of Swiss chard cut into slivers, and the celery stick thinly sliced. Cook for a further 2 minutes.

Barley scone bread

175g (6oz; 1½ cups) barley flour
4 tbsp olive oil
50g (2oz; ½ cup) cashew nuts, chopped (optional)
4 tbsp water
sea salt

Preheat the oven to 160°C (310°F), Gas Mark 3.
   Mix together all the ingredients to form a large scone. Divide it into four pieces. Place on a greased baking tray and bake for 20 to 25 minutes.

Millet and cashew nut risotto

225g (8oz; 1 cup) millet, cooked
125g (4oz; 1 cup) cashew nuts
50g (2oz; ½ cup) black olives (preservative-free)
2 sticks celery, sliced

Blanch the sliced celery by immersing it in boiling water for ½ minute. Mix the ingredients together and serve hot or cold.

Melon, cucumber and strawberry salad

1 honeydew melon, cut into cubes
½ cucumber, cut in half and sliced
225g (8oz; 2 cups) strawberries, sliced
1 small lettuce, shredded
pumpkin seeds
cold-pressed olive oil
sprigs of fresh mint to garnish

Place the shredded lettuce on a serving dish and arrange the other ingredients on top. Sprinkle with oil and garnish with mint.

Day 11

Introduce and test quail and quails' eggs. If you have had no adverse reaction to testing rice on Day 9 you can now start using it again in your diet. Also introduce and test the following food families (*except foods already tested): **lily family** (onion, garlic, asparagus, chives, leeks); **citrus family** (lemon, orange, grapefruit, lime, tangerine, citron); *****blueberry family** (blueberry, cranberry); *****laurel family** (avocado, cinnamon, bay leaves); *****beech family** (chestnuts and chestnut flour); *****birch family** (filberts, hazelnuts). You can also introduce **orange juice** and *****rice syrup**.

Suggested menu

Breakfast: Fresh grapefruit.
Millet porridge, blueberry muffins.
Poached quails' eggs with sweet potato or yam.
Main meal: Roasted quails with spring onion rice and cranberry sauce, served with green vegetables.
Brussels sprouts with chestnuts, served with millet.
Quails' egg and pasta salad with a French dressing.
Light meal: Cream of asparagus soup.
Avocado pear with French dressing.

Blueberry muffins

125g (4oz; 1 cup) millet flour or rice flour
125g (4oz; 1 cup) chestnut flour
4 quails' eggs, beaten
125g (4oz; 1 cup) blueberries
4 tbsp maple syrup
125ml (¼ pint; ½ cup) olive oil
1 tsp cream of tartar
½ tsp bicarbonate of soda
½ tsp cinnamon

Preheat the oven to 150°C (300°F), Gas Mark 2.

Mix all the ingredients together and fill six well-oiled muffin tins with the mixture. Bake for 20 minutes until firm.

Roasted quails with spring onion rice and cranberry sauce

6–8 oven ready quails (allow 1–2 per person)
sea salt

SPRING ONION RICE:
175g (6oz; 1½ cups) long grain rice (a little wild rice may be
    used)
125g (4oz; 1 cup) spring onions
800ml (1¾ pints; 3½ cups) water
2 bay leaves

FOR THE SAUCE:
225g (8oz; 2 cups) cranberries
125ml (¼ pint; ½ cup) water
1 clove garlic (optional)
zest and juice of 1 orange (optional)
2 tbsp maple syrup or to taste
pinch of cinnamon
1 tbsp fruit sugar

Preheat the oven to 180°C (350°F), Gas Mark 4.

Place the quails in a casserole dish and sprinkle with salt. Cover and cook for 30 minutes.

To cook the rice, cut the spring onions into 2cm (1in) lengths and place in a pan with the rice, bay leaves, salt and water. Bring to the boil, cover and simmer for 20 to 25 minutes until cooked. Remove the bay leaves before serving.

To make the cranberry sauce, place all the ingredients, except for the sugar, in a pan and simmer gently for 2 to 3 minutes until the cranberries are tender. Add fruit sugar to taste.

Place the rice on a serving dish and arrange the quails on top. Serve with cranberry sauce.

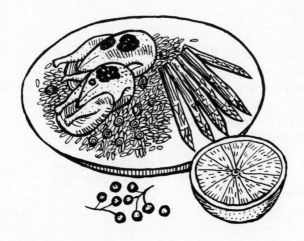

Brussels sprouts with chestnuts

450g (1lb; 4 cups) Brussels sprouts
450g (1lb; 4 cups) whole chestnuts
1 leek, sliced
zest of 1 lemon
1 tbsp chopped parsley
sea salt

If you are using dried chestnuts, these will need to be soaked overnight before cooking. Cook the chestnuts and lemon zest in boiling salted water for 15 minutes until tender.

Steam or boil the Brussels sprouts and leeks together for 5 to 7 minutes and drain. Add to the chestnuts and serve garnished with chopped parsley.

Quails' egg and pasta salad

250g (8oz; 4 cups) buckwheat pasta spirals
2 tsp olive oil
6–8 quails' eggs, hard boiled and cut in half
3 sticks celery, sliced
125g (4oz; 1 cup) celeriac, cut into strips and blanched
125g (4oz; 1 cup) asparagus tips
50g (2oz; ½ cup) walnuts
1 tbsp dill

Cook the pasta in boiling water until *al dente* (cooked but not soft), adding a little oil to the water to prevent sticking. Drain and allow to cool on a serving dish. Mix in the celeriac, celery, asparagus tips and walnuts and arrange the eggs on the top. Pour over a little French dressing and garnish with dill.

French dressing

juice of 2 lemons
125ml (¼ pint; ½ cup) cold-pressed virgin olive oil or walnut oil
1 tsp ground mustard
1 clove garlic, crushed
1 tsp fresh mint, chopped
½ tsp sea salt

Combine all the ingredients in a jar and shake well.

Cream of asparagus soup

450g (1lb; 4 cups) asparagus
1 litre (1¾ pints; 4 cups) game or vegetable stock or water
50g (2oz; ½ cup) ground almonds
1 large onion, chopped
juice of 1 lemon
1 tbsp fresh parsley, chopped
sea salt

Wash and prepare the asparagus. Cut off the tips and trim off the coarse outer parts of the remaining stems. Cut the stems into 2cm (1in) pieces. The tips are not needed in this recipe.

Discard the tips but cook the chopped onion and the asparagus stems in some stock or water for 5 to 7 minutes until soft. Make up the quantity of liquid with the stock and add the ground almonds and salt.

Liquidize the soup to a creamy consistency, add the lemon juice and garnish with chopped parsley.

Day 12

Introduce **barley**, and test and introduce the following (*except foods already tested): **beef; veal; potato family** (potato, tomato, aubergine (eggplant), peppers, paprika, cayenne, chilli); *****palm family** (coconut, date, date syrup); *****grapes, raisins** and **sultanas;** *****seaweed;** *****sesame seeds** and spread (tahini), *****sesame seed oil.**

Suggested menu

Breakfast: Grapes.
Rice porridge with prunes.
Barley or rice and sesame seed snacks.
Main meal: Beef stew and barley dumplings, served with mashed potatoes and peas.
Vegetable goulash with barley dumplings.
Light meal: Cream of tomato soup with barley scone bread.
Green pepper and pine nut pizza with salad.

Barley or rice and sesame seed snacks

125g (4oz; 1 cup) barley or rice flour
1 tbsp sago or tapioca flour
125ml (¼ pint; 1 cup) water
2 tbsp tahini
1 tbsp sesame seeds
2 tbsp sesame seed oil
1–2 tbsp honey
1tsp ground cinnamon

Preheat the oven to 150°C (300°F), Gas Mark 2.

Mix all the ingredients together with enough water to make a piping consistency. Place the mixture in a piping bag fitted with a large nozzle, and pipe out shapes onto a lined baking tray. Bake for 30 minutes.

Savoury snacks can be made by substituting the honey and cinnamon for ½ teaspoon cardamom, 1 teaspoon of dried herbs and a pinch of sea salt.

Beef stew and barley dumplings

FOR THE DUMPLINGS:
225g (8oz; 2 cups) barley flour
1 tsp cream of tartar
½ tsp bicarbonate of soda
75ml (3 floz; ⅓ cup) dripping or olive oil
cold water to mix

FOR THE STEW:
450g (1lb) organically reared beef steak, cubed
2 carrots, diced
1 parsnip, diced
2 sticks celery, sliced
½ litre (1 pint; 2 cups) stock or water
2 sprigs fresh thyme (or ½ tsp dried)
sea salt

Preheat the oven to 150°C (300°F), Gas Mark 2.

To make the dumplings, mix the ingredients together with a little cold water and mould into four balls.

To make the stew, bring the stock or water to boiling point in an ovenproof casserole dish and add the beef, vegetables, herbs and salt, and return to boiling point. Add the barley dumplings and place the casserole in the oven and cook for 1½ hours until the meat is tender.

Vegetable goulash

225g (8oz; 2 cups) tomatoes, skinned and chopped
125g (4oz; 1 cup) French beans, cut into 2.5cm (1in) lengths
125g (4oz; 1 cup) potatoes, cut into even sized chunks
2 carrots, sliced
2 sticks celery, sliced
½ litre (1 pint; 2 cups) water
1 tbsp tomato purée
2 tbsp sunflower oil
sprig of rosemary or thyme
sea salt or kelp
barley dumplings (see page 62)

Place all the vegetables and the water in a heavy-based pan and bring to the boil. Add the tomato purée, water, seasoning and dumplings and cook gently for 40 minutes. Remove the sprig of rosemary or thyme, stir in the oil and serve.

Cream of tomato soup

450g (1lb; 4 cups) fresh tomatoes, skinned, quartered
    and seeded
1 carrot, chopped
1 potato, chopped
1 tbsp tomato purée
½ litre (1 pint; 2 cups) stock or water
sea salt
sunflower oil
1 tbsp fresh basil

Boil the vegetables in stock or water in order of cooking time. Allow them to cool a little and then liquidize. Reheat, adding the remaining stock, and cook for 2 minutes. Stir in some cold-pressed sunflower oil just before serving and garnish with basil.

NB Purchase tomato purée in a glass jar and check the label to make sure that there are no other added ingredients.

Green pepper and pine nut pizza

FOR THE DOUGH:
225g (8oz; 2 cups) barley flour (or rice flour)
225g (8oz; 2 cups) swede, cooked and mashed
½ cup olive oil
sea salt

FOR THE SAUCE:
225g (8oz; 2 cups) fresh tomatoes, skinned and chopped
1 zucchini, grated
2 tbsp tomato purée
sea salt

FOR THE TOPPING:
50g (2oz; ½ cup) pine nuts
1 large green pepper, de-seeded and sliced
6 black olives, stoned and halved
1 tsp dried oregano

Preheat the oven to 160°C (310°F), Gas Mark 3.

To prepare the dough, mix all the ingredients together and mould into four individual rounds or press into a well-oiled rectangular baking tray.

For the sauce, cook the tomatoes, zucchini, tomato paste and salt and spoon onto the dough bases.

Top with pine nuts, olives and slices of pepper, and sprinkle with oregano. Bake for 20 to 25 minutes.

Day 13

Introduce and test the following (*except foods already tested): **soya** and **soya bean products** (soya flour, soya milk, soya dried milk, soya oil, soya meat substitutes, tofu, tempeh, soya egg replacer, tamari soya sauce); **wild boar** and **outdoor-reared pork**; **sugar-free jams** made with apple juice and pectin; **mushrooms** (including wild porcini, oyster and shiitake); ***mustard seed**.

Suggested menu

Breakfast: Fresh apples.
Rice porridge with stewed apples and raisins and soya milk.

Main meal: Wild boar cutlets with mushroom sauce, served with French beans and yam.
Pork, apple and chestnut pie (soya mince may be substituted for pork), served with seasonal vegetables or salad.

Light meal: Yellow split pea soup.
Mushroom and smoked tofu kebabs with fresh salad.

Wild boar cutlets with mushroom sauce

4–6 wild boar lean cutlets, trimmed
225g (8oz; 2 cups) small turnips, diced
125g (4oz; 2 cups) button mushrooms
½ litre (1 pint; 2 cups) stock
1 tsp ground mustard seeds
sea salt
sago or tapioca flour

Grill the cutlets on both sides to seal the juices. Place in a pan with the turnips and seasoning and bring to the boil. Cover and simmer for 30 minutes and then add the mushrooms. Cook for a further 5 minutes. Thicken the juices with a little tapioca or sago flour.

Pork, apple and chestnut pie

SWEET POTATO AND BUCKWHEAT PASTRY:
125g (4oz; 1 cup) sweet potato, baked and mashed
50g (2oz; ½ cup) buckwheat flour
50g (2oz; ½ cup) soya flour
½ cup olive oil
1 tsp baking powder (wheat-free)
sea salt
water to mix

FOR THE FILLING:
225g (8oz; 2 cups) minced pork
225g (8oz; 2 cups) chestnuts, cooked and broken into pieces
225g (8oz; 2 cups) eating apples, peeled and sliced
4 quails' eggs or 2 tbsp soya egg replacer, beaten
125ml (¼ pint; ½ cup) stock
1 tsp fresh thyme or ½ tsp dried
sea salt

Preheat the oven to 160°C (310°F), Gas Mark 3. Line and
grease a 20cm (8in) flan case.

Mix together the ingredients for the pastry and form into a
firm dough. Roll out two thirds of the pastry and line the base
of the flan case. Prick the base. Mix together all the
ingredients for the filling and spread over the base of the pie.
Cover with the remaining pastry and seal the edges. Brush
with a little beaten egg and pierce the lid of the pie to allow
steam to escape.

Bake for 50 minutes and serve hot or cold.

Yellow split pea soup

125g (4oz; ⅔ cup) yellow split peas, soaked
175g (6oz; 1½ cups) yam or sweet potato, diced
3 sticks celery, chopped
1 litre (1¾ pints; 4 cups) stock or water
1 tsp caraway seeds
1 bay leaf
sea salt
parsley to garnish

Allow the split peas to soak in hot water for 1 to 2 hours.
(Split peas are processed and will not sprout.) Cook the peas
gently in some of the water or stock with the seasoning for 40
minutes until beginning to turn soft. Remove the bay leaf.

Cook the celery and potatoes in some more of the water or
stock until soft. Add to the split peas and liquidize until
smooth. Return to the pan, add the remaining liquid and
reheat. Cook for 2 minutes and serve with a garnish of
chopped parsley.

Mushroom and smoked tofu kebabs

275g (10oz; 1¼ cups) smoked tofu
225g (8oz; 4 cups) button mushrooms
French dressing (see page 60)
lettuce leaves
fresh herbs to garnish

Cut the mushrooms into halves. Either use them raw or
quickly blanch them in boiling water.

Cut the tofu into 2.5cm (1in) cubes and thread onto a
wooden skewer, alternating each cube with a mushroom.
Prepare four skewers in this way, then arrange them on a bed
of lettuce leaves on a serving dish. Pour over the salad
dressing and garnish with fresh herbs.

Day 14

Test **oats** and introduce on Day 16. Introduce the following
(*except foods already tested): **freshwater fish** (salmon, trout,
pike, perch, bass); ***ginger family** (arrowroot, cardamom,
ginger, turmeric); ***nutmeg family** (nutmeg, mace).

Suggested menu

Breakfast: Fresh melon with ground ginger and fruit sugar.
　　　　　　　Pear and ginger fruit slice.
Main meal: Fresh salmon with raspberry coulis, served with
　　　　　　　rice and French beans.
　　　　　　　Cardamom nut rice with fresh green salad.

Light meal: Beetroot soup with oatcake biscuits.
Stuffed papayas.
Breadfruit with ginger and green peppers.

Pear and ginger fruit slice

2 pears, peeled, cored and thinly sliced
125g (4oz; 1 cup) barley flour
125g (4oz; 1 cup) ground almonds
125ml (¼ pint; ½ cup) sesame seed oil
2 tbsp honey to taste
1 tsp ground ginger
4 quails' eggs
1 tsp grated lemon zest

Preheat the oven to 150°C (300°F), Gas Mark 2.

Beat the eggs and mix in the other ingredients. Spoon into a well-oiled baking tin and cook for 30 to 35 minutes.

Fresh salmon with raspberry coulis

4 wild salmon fillets
225g (8oz; 2 cups) fresh raspberries
1 tbsp fruit sugar
125ml (¼ pint; ½ cup) water
sea salt

Poach the salmon fillets in a little water with salt added for 5–7 minutes.

Place the raspberries in a saucepan with the water and fruit sugar and bring to the boil. Simmer until the raspberries begin to break up. Liquidize, strain and serve with the salmon.

Cardamom nut rice

225g (8oz; 1 cup) organic long-grain rice
1 onion, chopped
1 clove garlic, crushed
1 tsp fresh ginger, finely grated
3 black cardamom pods, crushed
½ tsp ground cumin
½ tsp ground lemon grass
½ tsp turmeric

½ litre (1 pint; 2 cups) vegetable stock or water
50g (2oz; ½ cup) cashew nuts
50g (2oz; ½ cup) sultanas
50g (2oz; ½ cup) almonds, blanched and halved lengthways
50g (2oz; ½ cup) pumpkin seeds
2 tbsp olive oil
sea salt

Put the rice in a pan with the onion, garlic, spices, salt and stock or water and bring to the boil. Cover and simmer for 25 to 30 minutes until the rice is cooked.

Remove the cardamom pods from the rice and stir in the olive oil. Add the seeds, nuts and sultanas, and serve.

Beetroot soup

450g (1lb; 4 cups) uncooked beetroot, peeled and diced
350g (12oz; 3 cups) yam or potatoes, peeled and diced
1 stick celery, sliced
1 onion, sliced
1 litre (1¾ pints; 4 cups) stock or water
pinch of nutmeg
sea salt or kelp
parsley for garnishing

Place the vegetables in a pan with a little water and cook until tender. Cool slightly and then liquidize until smooth. Return to the pan, add the remaining stock, salt or kelp and nutmeg and bring to the boil. Cook for 3 to 5 minutes and serve garnished with chopped parsley.

Stuffed papayas

2 papayas
125g (4oz) trout (not farmed) or tofu
50g (2oz; ¼ cup) wild rice, cooked
25g (1oz; ¼ cup) pine kernels
juice of one lime
iceberg lettuce
alfalfa sprouts

Cut the papayas in half and discard the seeds. Grill the trout
for 2 to 3 minutes and leave to cool. Flake the trout and mix
with the pine nuts and wild rice. Spoon the mixture into the
hollow centres of the papayas and pour over the lime juice.
Place on individual plates and garnish with iceberg lettuce
and alfalfa sprouts.

Breadfruit with ginger and green peppers

1 breadfruit
2 green peppers, sliced
1 large pear, peeled, cored and sliced
3 cardamom pods, crushed
1 tsp ginger, grated
1 tbsp tahini
250ml (½ pint; 1 cup) water

Peel and core the breadfruit and cut into chunks. Steam for
30 minutes until tender.

For the sauce, put the peppers and pear in a pan with the
cardamom pods, ginger and water and cook until soft. Add
the tahini and liquidize until smooth.

Place the breadfruit on a serving dish and pour over the
sauce.

Day 15

Introduce and test the following (*except foods already tested): **turkey**; *myrtle family (allspice, cloves, guava); **black** and **white pepper** (this can be used uncooked, on cold food; when cooked, however, pepper can become an irritant and is not good for the liver); *Rooibosch tea (this African tea, available at healthfood stores and some supermarkets, is additive- and caffeine-free and low in tannin and may be made like ordinary tea and served with a slice of lemon). You can have quails' eggs again today, but do not use them again until you have tested ducks' eggs on Day 19. This is to give you a four-day gap.

Suggested menu

Breakfast: Freshly squeezed orange juice.
            Millet and buckwheat muesli.
            Poached or scrambled quails' eggs
Main meal: Turkey and mushroom fricassee with sautéed sweet potato and green salad.
            Cauliflower and chickpea curry with wholemeal basmati rice and sliced tomatoes.
Light meal: Onion and barley soup.
            Jacket potato with coleslaw salad.

Turkey and mushroom fricassee

450g (1lb) turkey fillet, cut into strips
225g (8oz; 4 cups) mushrooms, sliced
2 sticks celery, sliced
1 onion, chopped
½ litre (1 pint; 2 cups) game or vegetable stock
1 tbsp corn, barley or rice flour
½ tsp ground mustard
2 cloves
sea salt

Bring the stock to the boil and add the turkey, vegetables and seasoning. Cook gently for 10 to 15 minutes. Mix the flour with a little cold water and add to the pan to thicken the sauce.

Cauliflower and chickpea curry

225g (8oz; 1⅓ cups) chickpeas, sprouted and cooked
1 small cauliflower, broken into florets
225g (8oz; 2 cups) potatoes, diced
1 green pepper, seeded and sliced
2 sticks celery, chopped
1 large onion, sliced
2 cloves garlic, crushed
1 tsp ginger, grated
125g (4oz; ½ cup) creamed coconut
1 tbsp tomato purée
1 litre (1¾ pints; 4 cups) vegetable stock or water
2 tsp curry powder (wheat-free)
1 tbsp lemon juice
2 tbsp olive oil
sea salt

Warm the oil and a little water in a pan and gently cook the onion until transparent but not brown. Add the ginger, garlic and curry powder and cool-fry for 2 minutes, then add the coconut, tomato purée, stock and potatoes. Bring to the boil and simmer for 5 minutes. Add the remaining ingredients and cook for a further 15 minutes until the vegetables are tender.

Onion and barley soup

450g (1lb; 4 cups) onions, thinly sliced
125g (4oz; ½ cup) pot barley
1 litre (1¾ pints; 4 cups) game or vegetable stock or water
1 tbsp tamari soya sauce
1 bay leaf
olive oil
2oz dried arame seaweed, washed and soaked
chopped parsley

Place the onions, bay leaf and barley in a pan and cover with half the stock or water. Cook for 20 minutes until the barley is soft. Add the arame seaweed and soaking water and the remaining stock and bring to the boil. Simmer for a further 10 minutes. Remove the bay leaf. Stir in the olive oil and tamari sauce and garnish with chopped parsley.

Coleslaw

1 small white cabbage, shredded
225g (8oz; 2 cups) grated carrot
2 red apples, cored and diced
1 tbsp lemon juice
2 sticks celery, sliced
1 tbsp chives, chopped
75g (3oz; ¾ cup) raisins
2 tbsp mayonnaise (see page 74)
chopped fresh parsley

Toss the apple in lemon juice to prevent browning. Mix all the ingredients together, stir in the mayonnaise and sprinkle with parsley.

Mayonnaise

2 quails' egg yolks
1 whole quails' egg
1 tbsp lemon juice
125ml (¼ pint; ½ cup) walnut oil, olive oil or mixture
½ tsp ground mustard
pinch white pepper
sea salt

Make sure all the ingredients are at room temperature. Place the eggs, lemon juice and seasoning in a liquidizer and blend for a few seconds. Turn on to maximum speed and slowly pour in the oil until the mixture thickens.

Day 16

Test **corn** (cornflour, maize flour, sweetcorn) and introduce it on Day 18. You can introduce **oats**, providing that you have not had any adverse reactions. If you wish, you can introduce **barleycup, chicory** and **dandelion coffee** substitutes. Chicory and dandelion belong to the aster family.

Suggested menu

Breakfast: Fresh fruit, oat milk.
              Oatflake porridge.
              Date and coconut muesli bars.
Main meal: Shoulder of lamb with apricot, raisin and oat
              stuffing, served with new potatoes and seasonal
              green vegetables.
              Olive and aubergine flan, served with arame
              seaweed with sesame seeds and fresh green salad.
Light meal: Miso soup with corn bread.
              Hummus or cannellini bean dip with crudités.

Oat milk

50g (2oz; ½ cup) oatmeal or flakes
1 litre (1¾ pints; 4 cups) water
1 tsp honey (optional)
drop of natural vanilla essence (optional)

Place the oats in a large pan with the water and bring to the boil. Simmer for 10 minutes. Cool slightly, liquidize until smooth and strain. Stir in honey and vanilla essence if desired. Serve hot or cold.

Date and coconut muesli bars

225g (8oz; 2 cups) dried dates, chopped
225g (8oz; 2 cups) rolled oats
225g (8oz; 1 cup) creamed coconut, warmed
2 tbsp water
125ml (¼ pint; ½ cup) sesame seed oil
zest of 1 orange (optional)

Preheat the oven to 160°C (310°F), Gas Mark 3.

Put the chopped dates and water in a pan and gently heat for 15 to 20 minutes until soft. Place in a food mixer and mix with the remaining ingredients. Turn into a well-oiled or lined baking tin and bake for 40 minutes. Allow to cool in the tin before cutting and transferring to a wire rack.

Shoulder of lamb with apricot, raisin and oat stuffing

1 boned shoulder of lamb

FOR THE STUFFING:
225g (8oz; 2 cups) fresh apricots, chopped
50g (2oz; ½ cup) raisins
50g (2oz; ½ cup) oat flakes
2 tsp fresh tarragon, parsley or another herb
1 tsp tapioca flour
250ml (½ pint; 1 cup) stock or water
sea salt

Preheat the oven to 180°C (350°F), Gas Mark 4.

Mix the apricots, raisins, oats and seasoning in a bowl and bind together with the tapioca flour and stock or water. Place the stuffing into the cavity of the meat and tie up with string or secure with skewers. Roast in the oven for 15 minutes, then reduce the temperature to 160°C (310°F), Gas Mark 3 and cook for a further 1½ hours.

Olive and aubergine flan

FOR THE PASTRY CASE:
125g (4oz; 1 cup) fine oatmeal
125g (4oz; 1 cup) rice flour
1 tbsp tapioca flour
125ml (¼ pint, ½ cup) olive oil
pinch of salt
water to mix

FOR THE FILLING:
2 aubergines, thinly sliced
1 green pepper, sliced and de-seeded
8–10 pitted green olives

FOR THE SAUCE:
275g (10oz; 1¼ cups) tofu
1 stick celery, sliced
1 onion, chopped
4 tbsp stock or water
1 tsp sago flour
sea salt or kelp

Preheat the oven to 150°C (300°F), Gas Mark 2.

To prepare the flan case, mix the ingredients together using a little cold water to make a firm dough. Roll out between two sheets of greaseproof paper or tough polythene and mould into the flan dish.

Sprinkle the sliced aubergines with salt and leave for 30 minutes to remove the bitterness. Rinse them, then drain and dry on kitchen paper. Steam or boil gently in a little water until soft, and arrange in the flan case with the green pepper and olives.

To make the sauce, gently steam the onion and celery, cool slightly and place in a liquidizer, together with the tofu, stock or water, cornflour and salt, and blend until smooth. Pour into the flan case and bake for 40 to 45 minutes until set.

Miso soup

4 spring onions, sliced
1 clove garlic, crushed
1 tsp grated ginger
1 carrot, diced
½ small cauliflower, broken into florets
2 sheets nori seaweed, cut into 2.5cm (1in) squares
50g (2oz; ½ cup) peas
1 litre (1¾ pints; 4 cups) water
1 tbsp miso soya bean paste

Gently cook the vegetables and the ginger in the water until soft. Pour off a little of the water into a bowl and blend the miso in this. Then add the liquid to the vegetables but do not allow the soup to boil. Add the nori and serve.

Corn bread

175g (6oz; 1½ cups) maize flour
125g (4oz; 1 cup) cooked squash or pumpkin
1 tsp cream of tartar
½ tsp bicarbonate of soda
4 tbsp olive oil
125ml (¼ pint; ½ cup) water
2 tsp honey

Preheat the oven to 150°C (300°F), Gas Mark 2.

Mix all the ingredients together and place in a lined 1lb loaf tin. Bake for 40 to 45 minutes until firm.

Hummus

225g (8oz; 1⅓ cups) chickpeas, sprouted and cooked
4 tbsp tahini
juice of 2 lemons
2 cloves garlic
1 tbsp olive oil
1 tbsp sesame seed oil
black pepper
sea salt

TO GARNISH:
parsley
paprika pepper

Place all the ingredients in a food processor and mix until smooth, adding some of the chickpea cooking water if necessary.

Serve with crudités – sticks of carrot, celery, peppers, cauliflower florets, radishes, chicory leaves, etc.

Cannellini bean dip

Follow the recipe for hummus, using sprouted cannellini beans instead of chickpeas, and flavour with chopped fresh mint and ground cumin. Garnish with a sprig of mint.

Day 17

Test and introduce **yeast** and **green leaf tea** which is a china tea, low in caffeine and tannin. It is drunk without milk but may be served with lemon.

Suggested menu

Breakfast: Pears and rice porridge.
Barley muffins.

Main meal: Venison steak burgers with mixed vegetables and salad.

Rice and lentil loaf with fresh salad.

Light meal: Black bean and mushroom soup.

Rice, barley and bean sprout salad.

Barley muffins

125g (4oz; 1 cup) brown rice flakes
125g (4oz; 1 cup) barley flour
50g (2oz; ½ cup) sunflower seeds, chopped
50g (2oz; ½ cup) seedless raisins
250ml (½ pint; 1 cup) soya milk
2 tsp dried yeast
1 tsp fruit sugar
1 tsp arrowroot or sago flour
½ tsp cinnamon

Preheat the oven to 190°C (375°F), Gas Mark 5.

Soak the rice flakes in the soya milk for 5 minutes to soften them and then mix all the ingredients together and spoon into a lined loaf tin, filling it two-thirds full. Leave in a warm place to rise for 30 minutes.

Bake for 30 minutes until firm.

Venison steak burgers

450g (1lb) minced venison
50g (2oz; ½ cup) fine oatmeal or gram flour
125g (4oz; 1 cup) chestnut flour
1 tsp ground coriander
1 tsp chives, chopped
sea salt

Mix together all the ingredients. Shape into four burgers about 2cm (¾in) thick. Grill for 5 to 7 minutes on each side.
  These may be made up in larger quantities and frozen.

Rice and lentil loaf

225g (8oz; 1 cup) short grain brown rice, soaked and cooked
175g (6oz; 1 cup) brown or green lentils, sprouted and cooked
3 sticks celery, finely chopped
125g (4oz; 1 cup) walnuts, chopped
1 tsp sage, chopped
2 tsp chives, chopped
½ cup vegetable stock or water
1 tsp arrowroot, sago or tapioca flour
sea salt or kelp

Preheat the oven to 150°C (300°F), Gas Mark 2.
  Mix the ingredients together and pack into a well-oiled 1lb loaf tin and cook for 35 minutes until firm.

Black bean and mushroom soup

125g (4oz; 2 cups) wild mushrooms, diced
125g (4oz; ⅔ cup) black beans, soaked, sprouted and cooked
2 leeks, thinly sliced
1 litre (1¾ pints; 4 cups) stock or water
1 tbsp soya, gram or barley flour
1 bay leaf
sprig of thyme
sea salt

Steam the leeks until tender. Add the stock and bring to the boil. Mix in the mushrooms, flour, beans and seasoning and cook gently for 15 to 20 minutes.
  Remove the bay leaf and thyme and serve.

Rice, barley and bean sprout salad

175g (6oz; ¾ cup) cooked rice
50g (2oz; ¼ cup) cooked pot barley
175g (6oz; 1½ cups) French beans, sliced and cooked
125g (4oz; 1 cup) garden peas, cooked
125g (4oz; 1 cup) bean sprouts
2 spring onions, chopped (optional)
French dressing (see page 60)
4 heads of chicory or 1 bunch of watercress

Allow the cooked grains and vegetables to cool. Mix in with
the remaining ingredients and cover with the salad dressing.

Place in the centre of a serving dish and arrange chicory
leaves or watercress around the edge.

Day 18

Introduce corn providing you have not had any adverse
reactions. Test **rye** and introduce on Day 20. NB If you buy
rye or pumpernickel bread, check that it does not contain any
wheat. Introduce and test the **crustacean family** (crab,
crayfish, lobster, prawn, shrimp).

Suggested menu

Breakfast: Fresh melon.
Quinoa porridge with ginger syrup.
Main meal: Prawn, avocado and fennel salad with barley or
buckwheat pasta.
Stuffed green peppers, served with baby corn and
sugar peas.
Light meal: Sweet corn and lima bean succotash soup with
rye crackers.
Open sandwiches made with pumpernickel rye
bread.
Corn fritters.

Ginger syrup

125ml (¼ pint; ½ cup) water
1 tsp grated ginger
250ml (½ pint; 1 cup) white grape juice

Bring the water to the boil and add the ginger. Cook for 2 to 3 minutes and add to the grape juice. Continue cooking until the liquid is reduced by half. Strain and use hot or cold.

Prawn, avocado and fennel salad with buckwheat pasta

350g (12oz; 3 cups) peeled prawns
225g (8oz; 4 cups) buckwheat pasta
2 ripe avocado pears, sliced
1 bulb fennel, sliced
salad leaves
1 tsp dill
6–8 black olives
sprigs of thyme
French dressing (see page 60)

Cook the pasta until *al dente*. Drain and allow to cool.

Arrange the salad leaves on a serving dish and place the prawns, avocado pears, fennel and buckwheat pasta on top.

Spoon over the salad dressing, sprinkle with dill and garnish with sprigs of thyme and black olives.

Stuffed green peppers

4 large green peppers
175g (6oz) lean minced lamb or sprouted and cooked aduki
  beans.
175g (6oz; 1½ cups) cooked rice
450ml (¾ pint; 1¾ cups) stock
50g (2oz; ½ cup) chopped almonds
50g (2oz; ½ cup) chopped olives
1 onion, chopped
1 tomato, peeled and diced
1 tsp ground coriander seeds
½ tsp ground cinnamon
sea salt

Preheat the oven to 180°C (350°F), Gas Mark 4.

Prepare the peppers for stuffing by removing a piece from the top of each and scooping out the seeds. Mix the rest of the dry ingredients together and use it to stuff the peppers. Place the peppers in a baking dish, replace their tops and pour over the stock. Bake for 1 hour, basting from time to time.

Sweetcorn and lima bean succotash

125g (4oz; 1 cup) yam, diced
125g (4oz; 1 cup) zucchini, diced
2 sticks celery, sliced
175g (6oz; 1 cup) lima beans, sprouted and cooked
350g (12oz; 3 cups) sweetcorn kernels
1 sprig thyme
3 sage leaves, chopped
250ml (½ pint; 1 cup) vegetable stock or water
2 tbsp olive oil
sea salt

Cook the yam, followed by the zucchini and then the celery, until soft. Add the remaining ingredients and simmer for 10 minutes.

Open sandwiches

Spread slices of rye or pumpernickel bread with tahini, hummus or nut spread.

Fish salad – 1 sardine, 2 tomato wedges, lettuce leaf, cress and lemon slice.
Grape and tofu – slices of tofu, lettuce, tomato wedge, 1 or 2 black grapes halved and de-seeded.
Sprouted bean salad – alfalfa sprouts, cucumber slices, tomato wedge.
Potato salad – sliced cooked new potato, sliced radishes and cress.
Game bird – cold breast of pheasant, watercress, slice of fresh orange.
Egg and tomato – slices of hard-boiled quails' eggs, 3 slices tomato, lettuce and parsley.
Prawn salad – 50g (2oz; ½ cup) prawns, lettuce, 2 tomato wedges, lemon wedge and parsley.
Crab meat salad – 50g (2oz; ½ cup) crab meat, lettuce, 2 walnut halves, cress, black olive.

Corn fritters

175g (6oz; 1½ cups) cornflour
125g (4oz; 1 cup) sweetcorn
olive or sesame seed oil
½ tsp sea salt

Mash or liquidize the corn, add the flour and salt and mix with a little water. Cook as a small pancake on a hot griddle or cool-fry using a little olive or sesame seed oil.

Day 19

Test **duck** and **goose**, and **duck** and **goose eggs**, but do not introduce duck eggs into your diet until you have tested chicken eggs on Day 23. You can continue to have duck after today, though, provided you have had no adverse reactions.

Suggested menu

Breakfast: Orange and grapefruit salad.
Millet and buckwheat muesli.
Main meal: Roast duck with orange and grapefruit sauce,
crispy potatoes and runner beans or seasonal
vegetables.
Millet, hazelnut and tofu croquettes with tomato
sauce, served with vegetables.
Light meal: Celery and chestnut soup (see page 32)
Herb omelette with fresh salad.

Roast duck with orange and grapefruit sauce

1.8 kg (4lb) oven-ready duck
2 small grapefruit
3 oranges
2 tbsp honey
2 bay leaves
1 tsp cornflour or tapioca flour

Preheat the oven to 190°C (375°F), Gas Mark 5.

Prick the duck all over with a fork. Sprinkle with salt and
place half a grapefruit and two bay leaves in the body cavity.

Place the duck breast-side down on a rack or trivet in a
roasting pan and roast in the oven for 30 minutes. Reduce the
oven temperature to 160°C (310°F), Gas Mark 3, and cook for
a further 1½ hours, basting from time to time. You can also, if
you wish, remove the pan from the oven and pour off the
excess fat and use this for roasting potatoes.

To prepare the sauce, squeeze the juice from the remaining
grapefruit half and the juice from an orange. Peel the other
grapefruit and oranges and cut the peel into thin strips. Bring
some water to the boil and blanch the strips of peel for 2 to 3
minutes, drain and put to one side. Cut the oranges into thin
slices and divide the grapefruit into segments.

When the duck is cooked, pour off the cooking juices and
place it on a serving dish and keep warm.

Skim off the excess fat from the roasting pan. Place the
roasting pan over a medium heat. Mix the cornflour to a
smooth paste with a little cold water and add to the juices in

the pan. Add the orange and grapefruit juices, the strips of peel and the honey and simmer, stirring for 2 to 3 minutes until the sauce thickens. Pour round the duck. Garnish with the orange slices arranged along the breast and the grapefruit segments round the dish. Serve immediately.

Crispy roast potatoes

1 kg (2.2lb) potatoes
barley, corn or sago flour
dripping from the duck
sea salt

Peel and prepare the potatoes, scoring each piece. Place them in a large saucepan and pour over enough boiling water to cover, add some salt and bring to the boil. Place the lid on the pan and boil for 3 or 4 minutes.

Drain the potatoes in a colander. While still hot, use a spoon or some tongs to place a few at a time into the flour until all have been evenly coated. Place in a roasting pan with the warm fat from the duck and roast on the top shelf of the oven with the duck for 40 to 60 minutes until crisp and golden. (NB This is a treat – roasting is not advised too often.)

Millet, hazelnut and tofu croquettes

225g (8oz; 2 cups) millet flakes, cooked
275g (10oz; 1¼ cups) silken tofu
125g (4oz; 1 cup) ground hazelnuts
1 tbsp tamari soya sauce
1 tbsp fresh parsley, chopped
sea salt
2 tbsp millet flour

Preheat the oven to 160°C (310°F), Gas Mark 3.

Blend all the ingredients together and divide into eight croquettes. Roll them in the millet flour and bake for 25 minutes.

Tomato sauce

450g (1lb; 4 cups) tomatoes skinned, seeded and cut into chunks
2 sticks celery, chopped
1 clove garlic, crushed
4 spring onions, chopped
1 tbsp tomato purée
1 tbsp fresh basil, chopped
sea salt
2 tbsp sunflower or safflower oil

Gently steam the vegetables until soft. Add the tomato purée and basil and cook for a further minute. Stir in the oil before serving but do not heat.

Herb omelette

4 ducks' eggs
2 tbsp basil, chopped
2–3 chives, chopped
sea salt
olive oil and water for cool-frying

Crack the eggs into a basin and beat with a fork. Warm some water and oil in a small omelette pan and pour in the egg mixture.

Sprinkle in the chopped herbs and cook gently for approximately 1 minute until soft but no longer runny. Using a palette knife, fold the omelette in two and slip on to a hot plate.

Day 20

Test **sheep's milk products** but do not introduce them into your diet until after Day 28 when you will have tested cows' milk yoghurt and cheese. **Rye** can now be introduced, providing you are clear of any adverse reaction.

Suggested menu

Breakfast: Fresh fruit with sheep's milk yoghurt.
                Rye crackers with sheep's cheese and alfalfa sprouts.

Main meal: Creamy lamb with rye spaghetti with fresh green salad.
                Baked beans in tomato sauce, served with baked potatoes and fresh green salad.

Light meal: Leek and potato soup with rye bread.
                Greek salad.

Creamy lamb with rye spaghetti

450g (1lb) lean lamb, cut into strips
250ml (½ pint; 1 cup) lamb stock
1 large red pepper, cut into 5cm (2in) strips
225g (8oz; 2 cups) zucchini, cut into 5cm (2in) strips
275g (10oz; 1¼ cups) sheep's milk yoghurt

1 clove garlic
½ tsp ground rosemary
pinch of nutmeg
1 tbsp sago, tapioca or cornflour
sea salt
275g (10oz; 4–5 cups) rye spaghetti, barley or buckwheat pasta,
cooked

Pour the stock into a pan and bring to the boil. Add the lamb, vegetables and seasoning and cook gently for 15 minutes. Thicken with the flour if necessary.

Just before serving, stir in the yoghurt and serve with pasta.

Baked beans in tomato sauce

225g (8oz; 1⅓ cups) haricot beans, soaked and sprouted
1 carrot, diced
1 stick celery, diced
1 onion, chopped
1 clove garlic, crushed
225g (8oz; 2 cups) tomatoes skinned, deseeded and chopped
1 tbsp tomato purée
½ litre (1 pint; 2 cups) game stock or water
1 tsp ground cumin
1 tbsp chopped parsley
sea salt

Preheat the oven to 160°C (310°F), Gas Mark 3.

Place all the ingredients in a casserole dish and bake in the oven for 1½ hours.

Quick rye bread

1 cup rye flour
125ml (¼ pint; ½ cup) water
2 tbsp olive oil
pinch of salt

Preheat the oven to 180°C (350°F), Gas Mark 4.

Mix all the ingredients together and roll out on a well-greased or lined Swiss roll tin and cut into biscuits. Cook for 15 to 20 minutes.

Leek and potato soup

450g (1lb; 4 cups) potatoes, peeled and diced
3 leeks, sliced
1 litre (1¾ pints; 4 cups) stock or water
2 bay leaves
sprig of rosemary
bunch of chives, chopped
sea salt
creamed sheep's cheese or yoghurt (optional)

Gently cook the vegetables, bay leaves and rosemary in half of
the stock for 20 minutes. Remove the rosemary and bay
leaves. Allow to cool slightly and blend in a liquidizer. Add the
salt, and the remaining stock and chopped chives and reheat
gently.

The soup may be served with sheep's cheese or yoghurt,
stirred in at the last moment.

Greek salad

2 heads of chicory
1 small cos lettuce
4 tomatoes, halved and sliced
½ cucumber, diced lengthways
1 small red pepper, sliced
1 small green pepper,sliced
125g (4oz; 1 cup) pitted black olives
125g (4oz; ½ cup) ewe's milk feta cheese cut into cubes
1 tsp dried oregano
French dressing (see page 60)

Bunch the lettuce leaves together and cut into thin strips with
a sharp knife. Place on the bottom of a serving dish and
arrange the other ingredients on top.

Spoon over the dressing and sprinkle with oregano.

Day 21

Test **cane sugar** but do not introduce. Introduce and test **wine vinegar** and **water chestnuts**.

Suggested menu

Breakfast: Fresh fruit.
Compote of mixed dried fruit (figs, prunes, pears, apricots) with oat flakes.

Main meal: Pork tenderloin with prune, anchovy and almond stuffing, served with rice, carrots and peas.
Sweet and sour vegetables or pork served with wholemeal basmati rice.

Light meal: Green split pea soup with broccoli (see page 31).
Buckwheat and tomato stuffed mushrooms, served with red cabbage and orange salad.

Pork tenderloin with prune, anchovy and almond stuffing

2 outdoor-reared organic pork tenderloins
18 large prunes, soaked overnight
8 anchovy fillets
8 blanched almonds
1 tbsp arrowroot
½ litre (1 pint; 2 cups) vegetable or marrowbone stock
salt

Preheat the oven to 180°C (350°F), Gas Mark 4.

Remove the stones from the prunes. Stuff eight of them by wrapping anchovy fillets round blanched almonds and using them to fill the cavity of the prunes.

Prepare the tenderloins by slitting down one long side, just over half-way through, and open them out. Lay the stuffed prunes on one opened-out tenderloin. Lay the second tenderloin on top and tie together at intervals with string. Place in an ovenproof casserole, and bake for 40 minutes, reducing the oven temperature to 160°C (310°F), Gas Mark 3, after the first 20 minutes.

Cook the remaining prunes for 1 or 2 minutes. Drain and place on one side, keeping the liquid to add to the sauce.

Remove the pork tenderloin from the casserole, carve into slices and arrange on a hot serving dish. Use the cooking juices, stock and the prune juice to make a sauce, and thicken with arrowroot. Pour over the meat and garnish with the remaining prunes.

Sweet and sour vegetables with pork

450g (1lb) lean organic pork, cut into strips (optional)
225g (8oz; 2 cups) courgettes, sliced
225g (8oz; 2 cups) water chestnuts
125g (4oz; 1 cup) baby sweetcorn
125g (4oz; 1 cup) sugar peas
1 carrot cut into julienne strips
1 red or green pepper, sliced
½ cucumber, diced
2 tbsp sesame seed oil

FOR THE SAUCE:
2 tbsp soya sauce
2 tbsp wine vinegar
1 tbsp clear honey
1 tbsp tomato purée
125ml (¼ pint; ½ cup) water
2 tsp cornflour, tapioca or sago

Heat some water in the bottom of a wok and cook the pork. Add the vegetables and cook until just tender. Mix the honey, tomato purée and flour together and add the soya sauce, wine vinegar and water. Add the sweet and sour sauce tossing the vegetables until all are coated and the sauce thickens. Stir in the sesame seed oil, just before serving.

Buckwheat and tomato stuffed mushrooms

8 large flat mushrooms
FOR THE STUFFING:
175g (6oz; ¾ cup) raw buckwheat kernels, soaked
50g (2oz; ½ cup) sun-dried tomatoes, chopped (or 2 tbsp tomato purée)
2 onions, finely chopped
1 clove garlic, crushed
1 tbsp soya sauce
fresh basil, chopped

Preheat the oven to 160°C (310°F), Gas Mark 3.

Wash the mushrooms and remove the stems to use in the stuffing. Arrange the mushrooms on a well-oiled baking tray.

For the stuffing, chop the mushroom stalks and put in a saucepan with a little water, together with the tomatoes, onions, garlic, basil and drained buckwheat. Cover and simmer gently until cooked, stirring regularly. Add the soya sauce, and some water if necessary, and mix to make a firm paste.

Place a spoonful of the mixture onto the gills of each mushroom and bake in the oven for 15 to 20 minutes. Serve hot.

This mixture may also be used for stuffing marrows, zucchini, squash, aubergines and peppers.

Red cabbage and orange salad

225g (8oz; 2 cups) red cabbage, shredded
1 bulb fennel, sliced
2 oranges, peeled
1 bunch watercress
fresh dill

Divide the oranges into segments and cut each one into two or three pieces. Mix with the cabbage, watercress and fennel and sprinkle with sprigs of dill.

Day 22

Test **wheat**, (spelt wheat and kamut if available) and introduce on Day 24, providing that you have had no adverse reactions. Spelt wheat is an ancient precursor of modern-day wheat and is often more easily tolerated. Kamut is an ancient, non-hybridized grain, now being produced in the United States and slowly coming on to the market in Great Britain. It is a variety of high-protein, low-gluten wheat. It is usually tolerated well by 'wheat-allergic' people.

Introduce and test the **mollusc family** – abalone, snail, squid, clam, mussel, oyster, scallop, octopus.

Suggested menu

Breakfast: Fresh fruit.
Lamb burgers (see page 34).
Main meal: Seafood paella with fresh green salad.
Vegetable and lentil dahl with bulgur wheat (for testing) or millet.
Light meal: Pumpkin (or squash) soup with organic wholemeal bread (for testing).
Tortillas with bean and tomato filling, served with fresh green salad.

Seafood paella

(Serves 6–8)
450g (1lb; 4 cups) fresh mussels
350g (12oz; 1½ cups) long-grain rice
1 tsp ground lemon grass
1 onion, peeled and chopped
2 cloves garlic, crushed
2 tbsp olive oil
1 litre (1¾ pints; 4 cups) water or vegetable stock
450g (1lb; 4 cups) small squid, cleaned, prepared and cut into
  rings
175g (6oz; 1½ cups) prepared scallops
225g (8oz; 2 cups) tomatoes, skinned and chopped
1 red pepper de-seeded and sliced
125g (4oz; 1 cup) peas
1 bay leaf
125g (4oz; 1 cup) black olives (preservative-free)
1 lemon, cut into wedges
2 tsp fresh coriander, chopped

Scrub the mussels in cold water, removing the thread-like
beards. Discard any mussels that do not close when tapped.
Place in a pan with water and a bay leaf and cook for 5
minutes until the shells open. Strain off the liquid and make
up to 1 litre (1¾ pints; 4 cups) with water or vegetable stock.
Reserve eight to ten mussels in their shells and shell the rest,
discarding any that have not opened.

Warm the oil and a little water in a large shallow saucepan or paella pan and cool-fry the onion and garlic until soft. Stir in the rice and cook for 1 to 2 minutes. Add the stock, salt and lemon grass and liquid, bring to the boil and cook for 15 minutes. Stir in the tomatoes, red pepper, peas, squid, scallops and shelled mussels and cook for 4 to 5 minutes until the rice is tender. Serve garnished with mussels in their shells, black olives, wedges of lemon and a sprinkling of coriander leaves.

Vegetable and lentil dahl

125g (4oz; ⅔ cup) green lentils, sprouted
½ litre (1 pint; 2 cups) stock or water
1 onion, chopped
1 pepper, de-seeded and chopped
2 sticks celery, chopped
2 carrots, chopped
1 tsp ground cumin
1 tsp ground coriander
2 bay leaves
sea salt or kelp

Pour the stock into a saucepan and bring to the boil. Add the lentils, vegetables and seasoning and return to the boil. Simmer for 20 minutes until all the vegetables are tender. Remove the bay leaves and serve on a bed of millet or bulgur wheat.

Bulgur wheat

225g (8oz; 1 cup) bulgur wheat
½ litre (1 pint; 2 cups) boiling water
pinch of sea salt

Place the bulgur wheat in a bowl with the salt and pour over the boiling water. Leave for 15 to 20 minutes until all the water has been absorbed.

Pumpkin soup

675g (1½lb; 6 cups) pumpkin or squash, peeled, de-seeded and diced
1 litre (1¾ pints; 4 cups) stock or water

2 sticks celery, sliced
1 onion, sliced
1 tbsp chestnut flour
pinch of nutmeg
sea salt
2 tbsp safflower oil

Cook the onion, celery and pumpkin pieces in a little water. Add the stock, bring to the boil and simmer for 20 minutes. Blend in a liquidizer or rub through a fine sieve.

Return to the saucepan, add the chestnut flour, nutmeg, salt and more water as required. Bring to the boil and cook for a further 3 minutes. Stir in the oil before serving.

Tortillas with bean and tomato filling

FOR THE FILLING:
225g (8oz; 1⅓ cups) pinto beans, cooked and mashed
4 tomatoes, skinned and chopped
1 tbsp tomato purée
1 onion, chopped
2 cloves garlic, crushed
2 tsp fresh oregano
sea salt

FOR THE TORTILLAS:
175g (6oz; 1½ cups) maize flour
250ml (½ pint; 1 cup) warm water
1 tbsp olive oil
½ tsp sea salt

Steam the tomatoes, onion and garlic until soft. Mix with the mashed beans, tomato purée and seasoning.

Put the maize flour and salt in a bowl and gradually beat in the water and oil. Knead until a smooth, elastic dough is formed. Divide into eight portions and roll out each one between two sheets of greaseproof paper or tough polythene to form a thin round about 15cm (6in) in diameter. Cook in an ungreased frying pan for 2 or 3 minutes on each side.

Spoon 2 or 3 tablespoons of filling into each tortilla, fold over and serve.

Day 23

Introduce and test **chicken** and **chicken eggs**. Providing that you have not experienced any adverse reactions, you can now use all eggs, including quail and duck, in your diet.

Suggested menu

Breakfast: Fresh fruit.
                Tropical fruit muesli.
                Boiled egg.
Main meal: Curried chicken with chappatis, rice and sliced
                tomatoes or pineapple chunks.
                Sweet potato and parsnip bakes, served with
                fresh green salad.
Light meal: Garden vegetable soup.
                Avocado sweet and sour salad.

Curried chicken with chappatis

675g (1½ lb) chicken fillet pieces
275g (10oz; 2½ cups) onions, chopped
4 tbsp olive oil
125g (4oz; ½ cup) creamed coconut
½ litre (1 pint; 2 cups) chicken stock or water
1 large unripe banana, sliced
2 cloves garlic, crushed
1 tsp fresh ginger, mashed
1 tbsp curry leaves, crushed
1 tsp ground coriander
1 tsp ground cumin
1 tsp turmeric
sea salt
FOR THE CHAPPATIS:
175g (6oz; 1½ cups) barley, rye, buckwheat or rice flour
water

Warm the oil and a little water in a heavy-based saucepan and seal the chicken pieces on both sides. Take out, place on a plate and keep warm.

Gently cool-fry the onions in the oil and water until transparent. Sprinkle in the spices, then add the creamed coconut, garlic, ginger and salt. Return the chicken pieces to the pan, add the stock and finally the sliced banana. Cover with a lid and simmer for 35 minutes, turning the chicken occasionally.

To make the chappatis, mix the flour with water to make a firm dough. Break off small pieces and roll out into very thin rounds. Cook in a dry frying pan until brown and then grill under a hot grill until they puff up.

Sweet potato and parsnip bakes

450g (1lb; 4 cups) cooked sweet potato, mashed
225g (8oz; 2 cups) cooked parsnips, mashed
1 large onion, finely chopped
1 clove garlic, crushed
1 tsp ground mustard seed
1 tbsp fresh parsley, chopped
sea salt
1 tbsp sesame seeds for coating

Preheat the oven to 160°C (310°F), Gas Mark 3.

Mix the ingredients together and form into cakes. Roll in the sesame seeds and bake for 25 minutes.

Garden vegetable soup

175g (6oz; 1½ cups) small pickling onions
175g (6oz; 1½ cups) broccoli florets
2 carrots, thinly sliced
2 zucchini, diced
125g (4oz; 2 cups) button mushrooms, quartered
1 litre (1¾ pints; 4 cups) stock or water
1 tbsp barley or gram flour
sea salt or kelp
fresh thyme to garnish

Pour the stock or water into a pan and bring to the boil. Add all the ingredients, bring to boiling point and simmer until cooked. Garnish with fresh thyme.

Avocado sweet and sour salad

2 avocado pears, cut into chunks
lemon juice
225g (8oz; 2 cups) carrots, finely shredded
225g (8oz; 2 cups) mung bean sprouts
juice of two oranges
2 oranges, divided into segments
50g (2oz; ½ cup) organic sultanas

FOR THE DRESSING:
juice of one lemon
2 tbsp sweet almond oil
ground ginger
sea salt
black pepper

TO GARNISH:
julienne strips of orange peel

Sprinkle the avocado pear with lemon juice to prevent it from turning brown. Mix all the salad items together in a bowl. Mix the dressing ingredients together and pour over the salad. Garnish with strips of orange peel.

Day 24

Introduce and test **goats' milk products** (goats' milk, cheese and live yoghurt).

Suggested menu

Breakfast: Fresh fruit with goats' milk yoghurt.
Scrambled egg on toast.

Main meal: Chilli con carne, served with long-grain rice and fresh green salad.
Lamb or vegetable moussaka with fresh green salad.

Light meal: Cream of artichoke soup.
Buckwheat pasta with cheese and almond sauce.

Chilli con carne

450g (1lb) organic lean beef steak, cut into cubes
175g (6oz; 1 cup) red kidney beans, sprouted and cooked
6 tomatoes, skinned and chopped
2 onions, chopped
2 cloves garlic, crushed
½ litre (1 pint; 2 cups) stock
½ tsp ground chilli pepper
1 tsp oregano
1 tbsp barley or rice flour
sea salt

Pour the stock into a heavy-based saucepan and bring to the boil. Add all the ingredients except the tomatoes, kidney beans and flour. Cover and cook for 1 hour or until the meat is tender.

Add the tomatoes and kidney beans and cook for a further 15 minutes. Mix the barley flour with a little cold water and stir into the juices to thicken.

Moussaka

4 large aubergines sliced
450g (1lb) lean minced lamb or 225g (8oz; 1 cup) aduki beans,
sprouted and cooked
225g (8oz; 2 cups) tomatoes, skinned and chopped
1 tbsp tomato purée
2 large onions, chopped
1 clove garlic, crushed
1 green pepper, de-seeded and chopped
½ tsp oregano
2 tbsp sesame seed oil
sea salt or kelp

FOR THE SAUCE:
250ml (½ pint; 1 cup) goats' milk yoghurt
50g (2oz; ½ cup) hard goats' cheese, grated
2 free-range eggs or soya egg replacer
½ tsp ground mustard
½ tsp allspice or nutmeg
sea salt to taste

Preheat the oven to 160°C (310°F), Gas Mark 3.

Sprinkle the aubergine slices with salt to remove bitterness. Leave for 30 minutes, then rinse, drain and dry on kitchen paper. Steam or boil in a little water until tender and set to one side.

Cool-fry the onions and garlic in oil and water until transparent. Add the lamb or aduki beans, tomatoes, pepper and flavourings and cook for 10 minutes.

Arrange the aubergine slices and the lamb or aduki bean mixture in layers in a well-oiled shallow ovenproof baking dish.

Beat together the eggs and yoghurt and add the spices and salt. Pour over the top of the moussaka and sprinkle with grated cheese. Bake for 30 to 40 minutes.

Cream of artichoke soup

(Jerusalem artichokes are in season from November to June.)
675g (1½lb; 6 cups) Jerusalem artichokes, peeled and sliced
1 litre (1¾ pints; 4 cups) chicken, game or vegetable stock
1 large onion, sliced
pinch of nutmeg
125ml (¼ pint; ½ cup) goats' milk yoghurt
sea salt

TO GARNISH:
sprigs of watercress or tarragon, freshly chopped

Pour the stock into a saucepan and bring to the boil. Add the artichokes, onion and seasoning and return to the boil. Cover and simmer for 20 minutes until the artichokes are tender.

Cool slightly and liquidize until smooth. Re-heat and stir in the yoghurt. Garnish with watercress or tarragon.

Buckwheat pasta with cheese and almond sauce

350g (12oz; 5–6 cups) buckwheat pasta (wheat-free)
sea salt

FOR THE SAUCE:
125g (4oz; 1 cup) ground almonds
275g (10oz; 1¼ cups) natural goats' yoghurt
pinch of nutmeg
sea salt

TO GARNISH:
125g (4oz; ½ cup) hard goats' cheese, grated
50g (2oz; ½ cup) blanched almonds
chopped parsley, tarragon or mint

Cook the buckwheat pasta in plenty of boiling, salted water until tender without being too soft or sticky. Drain and keep warm on a serving dish.

Mix together the sauce ingredients and pour over the pasta. Garnish with the almonds, grated cheese and a sprinkling of your chosen herb.

Day 25

Test **tea** and **cider vinegar**. You can also test **peanuts**, but take care not to eat too many because they may contain carcinogenic substances made by a fungus to which they are very susceptible.

Suggested menu

Breakfast: Fresh apple, pear or lychees.
Cornflakes (organic) with soya or nut milk.

Main meal: Fruit-roasted leg of wild boar with mashed potato, baked red cabbage and garden peas.
Root vegetable crumble with baked red cabbage and green vegetables.

Light meal: Celery and zucchini soup (see page 31).
Buckwheat and cashew nut burgers with fennel and bean sprout salad (see page 37) and tofu mayonnaise.

Fruit-roasted leg of wild boar

(Serves 8–10)
1.6–2kg (3½–4½lb) whole leg of wild boar
½ litre (1 pint; 2 cups) prune juice
arrowroot (optional)
FRUIT COATING:
175g (6oz; 1½ cups) dried apricots, finely chopped
175g (6oz; 1½ cups) dried prunes, finely chopped
10 juniper berries, crushed
grated zest and juice of 1 orange
2 tbsp oatmeal
1 tsp allspice
sea salt

Preheat the oven to 180°C (350°F), Gas Mark 4.

Mix together the ingredients for the fruit coating, using a little of the prune juice to bind if necessary.

Trim off the skin and any excess fat from the leg and place, inner side down, in a well-oiled roasting pan. Coat the upper surface with the fruit mixture, pressing it down evenly as you go. Pour the prune juice around the joint and cook for 40 minutes per 450g (1lb) weight. Reduce the temperature to 160°C (310°F), Gas Mark 3, after the first 20 minutes. Baste with the prune juice from time to time, until thoroughly cooked.

Transfer the meat to a warm serving dish. Add some water to the roasting pan and boil up the juices. Skim off any fat, thicken with arrowroot or similar flour if you wish, and serve with the meat.

Root vegetable crumble

FOR THE CRUMBLE:
125g (4oz; 1 cup) barley, rye or wheat flour
50g (2oz; ½ cup) chestnut flour
50g (2oz; ½ cup) rolled oats
50g (2oz; ½ cup) sunflower seeds, chopped
50g (2oz; ½ cup) hazelnuts, chopped
125ml (¼ pint, ½ cup) olive oil
1tsp fresh parsley, chopped
sea salt

FOR THE FILLING:
450g (1lb; 4 cups) in total of any of the following vegetables,
  diced: yam or sweet potato, turnip, carrots, parsnip, swede
2 leeks, sliced (optional)
2 sticks celery, sliced
15cm (6in) strip kombu seaweed
250ml (½ pint; 1 cup) vegetable stock
1 bay leaf
pinch of nutmeg
2 tsp arrowroot or cornflour
sea salt to taste

Preheat the oven to 160°C (310°F), Gas Mark 3.

Pour the stock into a saucepan. Bring to the boil and add the vegetables and seasoning. Return to the boil and then cover and simmer until tender.

Mix the arrowroot with a little cold water and add to the vegetables to thicken the juices. Remove the bay leaf and place the vegetable mixture in an ovenproof dish.

Make the crumble by lightly working the oil into the flour and rolled oats with your fingertips. Add the seeds, nuts and parsley and mix together. Sprinkle over the vegetables and bake for 25 to 30 minutes.

Baked red cabbage

(Serves 8–10)
1 kg (2.2lb; 8 cups) red cabbage, shredded
2 dessert apples, diced
1 large onion, sliced
2 cloves garlic, crushed
25g (1oz; ¼ cup) raisins
25g (1oz; ¼ cup) dates, chopped
2 tbsp cider vinegar
½ tsp ground cinnamon
½ tsp ground cloves
125ml (¼ pint; ½ cup) water
sea salt

Preheat the oven to 140°C (275°F), Gas Mark 1.

Arrange half the cabbage in an ovenproof casserole dish. Add the apple, onion, garlic, raisins and dates and then cover with the remaining cabbage. Mix the cider vinegar, salt, water and spices together and pour over the cabbage. Cover and cook slowly for 2 hours. This dish can be frozen.

Buckwheat and cashew nut burgers

125g (4oz; 1 cup) buckwheat flakes
125g (4oz; 1 cup) chopped cashew nuts
1 large carrot, finely grated
50g (2oz; ½ cup) gram flour
1 tsp ground cardamom
freshly chopped parsley
sea salt
olive or sesame seed oil for cool-frying
mineral water to mix

Blend all the ingredients together, either by hand or in a food mixer, using a little water to bind it into a firm mixture. Mould into four burgers or use a burger press and gently cool-fry, using a little water with the oil, for 3 to 4 minutes on each side.

These may be made up in larger quantities for freezing.

Tofu mayonnaise

225g (8oz; 1 cup) silken tofu
1 clove garlic, crushed (optional)
2 tbsp olive or safflower oil
2 tbsp cider vinegar or lemon juice
pinch of white pepper
sea salt

Place all the ingredients in a liquidizer and blend until smooth.

Day 26

Test **cocoa**. Chocolate bars made from organically grown cocoa beans can be bought at most healthfood stores. Test and introduce **capers** and **vanilla**.

Suggested menu

Breakfast: Fresh fruit.
               Chocolate hazelnut biscuits.
Main meal: Pot-roast leg of lamb, served with mashed potato and broccoli.
               Kedgeree, served with fresh spinach and carrots.
               Millet, lentil and brazil nut loaf (see page 37) served with okra and apricot salad.
Light meal: Fish soup (see page 32) with rye bread.
               Salmon and tomato fishcakes.
               Prawn or tofu chow mein.

Chocolate hazelnut biscuits

225g (8oz; 2 cups) wheat flour or fine oatmeal
1 tsp cream of tartar
½ tsp bicarbonate of soda
125g (4oz; ½ cup) fruit sugar
50g (2oz; ½ cup) cocoa powder
50g (2oz; ½ cup) chopped hazelnuts
4 tbsp sesame seed oil
1 tsp natural vanilla essence

Preheat the oven to 150°C (300°F), Gas Mark 2.

Mix all the ingredients together and divide into pieces the size of a walnut. Place on a lined baking sheet and flatten with a fork dipped in cold water. Decorate with nuts. Bake for 20 minutes. Allow to cool before lifting on to a wire rack.

Pot-roast leg of lamb

1.8kg (4lb) leg of lamb
2 carrots, sliced
1 parsnip, sliced lengthways
2 sticks of celery, sliced
1 leek, sliced (optional)
1 tsp tomato purée (optional)
½ litre (1 pint; 2 cups) stock or water
3–4 sprigs of rosemary
sea salt
sago or tapioca flour (optional)

Preheat the oven to 180°C (350°F), Gas Mark 4.

Trim off any excess fat from the lamb, season with salt and lay the sprigs of rosemary over the joint. Place in a roasting pan and put in the oven for 15 minutes to seal.

Remove the lamb from the oven and transfer to a large casserole dish. Add the vegetables, tomato purée and stock or water and cover with the lid. Place back in the oven, reducing the temperature to 150°C (300°F), Gas Mark 2. Cook for a further 2 hours until very tender.

Place the lamb on a serving dish with the vegetables and keep warm. Strain off the juices, skimming off any excess fat. The juices can be thickened with sago, tapioca or any permissible flour, and then served with the lamb.

Kedgeree

450g (1lb) cooked flaked cod, haddock or other saltwater fish
175g (6oz; ¾ cup) wholemeal rice, cooked
1 large onion, peeled and chopped
1 green or red pepper, chopped
2 cloves garlic, crushed
1 tsp ginger, mashed, or ½ tsp ground ginger
2 tsp turmeric
1 tbsp freshly chopped parsley
2 tbsp sesame seed oil
juice of one lemon
sea salt or kelp

Gently cook the onion, garlic, ginger, tumeric and pepper in a
little water until soft. Stir in the fish and rice and when
thoroughly mixed and cooked through, turn onto a serving
dish. Stir in the oil, salt and lemon juice and garnish with
parsley.

Okra and apricot salad

450g (1lb; 4 cups) okra
225g (8oz; 2 cups) tomatoes, skinned and chopped
1 onion, sliced
1 clove garlic, crushed
1 tbsp tomato purée
125g (4oz; 1 cup) dried apricots, soaked and sliced
fresh basil, chopped
2 tbsp olive oil
sea salt

FOR GARNISHING:
2 oranges, thinly sliced
julienne strips of orange peel

Warm the oil and a little water in a pan and gently cool-fry
the onion and garlic until soft. Add the okra, tomatoes and the
remaining ingredients apart from the basil. Cover the pan and
cook gently for 20 minutes, adding more water if necessary.
Stir in the basil and turn on to a serving dish. Arrange the
orange slices around the rim of the dish and garnish with a
few julienne strips of orange peel. Serve cold.

Salmon and tomato fishcakes

225g (8oz) flaked cooked salmon
225g (8oz; 2 cups) cooked and mashed potato or yam
2–3 tomatoes, skinned and chopped
25g (1oz; ¼ cup) capers, chopped
1 onion, finely chopped
1 tsp arrowroot or tapioca flour
1 tbsp lemon juice or 1 tsp ground lemon grass
1 tsp thyme, dried
sea salt or kelp
2 tbsp maize or millet flour for coating

Preheat the oven to 160°C (310°F), Gas Mark 3.

Mix all the ingredients together and mould into four
fishcakes. Roll them in the maize flour. Bake for 25 minutes.

Prawn or tofu chow mein

25cm (10in) wakame seaweed
350g (12oz; 3 cups) shelled prawns or 350g (12oz; 1½ cups) tofu,
cut into squares
225g (8oz; 2 cups) vermicelli (rice noodles)
225g (8oz; 2 cups) bean sprouts
225g (8oz; 2 cups) water chestnuts, sliced
125g (4oz; 2 cups) organic mushrooms, sliced
2 carrots, thinly sliced diagonally
1 tbsp tamari soya sauce
125ml (¼ pint; ½ cup) vegetable stock
1 tbsp organic white wine (optional)
sesame seed oil

Wash and soak the wakame seaweed for 10 minutes. Drain
and cut into 2–3cm (1in) pieces. The soaking water may be
used to cook the noodles.

Bring the water to the boil and cook the vermicelli until just
soft. Drain well and place on a serving dish and keep warm.

Heat some water in a wok or saucepan and cook the
vegetables for 5 minutes. Add the stock, and wine if liked,
and bring to the boil. Add the prawns or tofu, seaweed and
soya sauce and cook for another 3 minutes.

Place on the serving dish in the centre of the noodles and
sprinkle with sesame seed oil.

Day 27

Test **coffee**. Use filtered organic coffee as instant coffee contains chemicals. Coffee is a stimulant and can increase any adverse response which may be occurring, so only drink in moderation, if at all.

Suggested menu

Breakfast: Avocado fruit cocktail.
                       Sprouted grain bread.
Main meal: Chicken noodle main meal soup.
                       Wild duck with pineapple (see page 36) served
                       with braised celery and broccoli.
                       Spanish omelette, served with boiled potatoes
                       and fresh green salad.
Light meal: Cold avocado and lime soup.
                       Broccoli with ginger and macadamia nuts, served
                       with couscous (or quinoa) salad.

Avocado fruit cocktail

2 avocado pears, peeled and sliced
125g (4oz; 1 cup) green seedless grapes
125g (4oz; 1 cup) strawberries

2 peaches, skinned and chopped
125ml (¼ pint; ½ cup) water
juice of 1 lemon
2 tbsp maple syrup

Cook the peaches in the water for 2 to 3 minutes until just soft and allow to cool. Strain off the juice and mix this with the lemon juice and maple syrup. Divide the peach pieces between four individual glass bowls and arrange the rest of the fruit on top and pour over the juice.

Sprouted wheat grain bread

450g (1lb; 2 cups) organic wheat grains
filtered water for sprouting
sea salt

Rinse the grains and leave to soak for 15 hours. Drain off the water and leave to sprout for two or three days until the grains have developed 2.5cm (1in) sprouts. Rinse them morning and evening.

Preheat the oven to 130°C (250°F), Gas Mark ½.

Place the sprouts in a meat mincer and grind to a fine texture. Add the salt and place in a well-oiled loaf tin and bake for 4 to 5 hours until the bread leaves the sides of the tin. This bread can also be cooked overnight on the lower shelf of a cooking range or stove.

Chicken noodle main meal soup

225g (8oz) free-range chicken breast
175g (6oz; 3 cups) rice noodles
½ litre (1 pint; 2 cups) stock
250ml (½ pint; 1 cup) coconut milk
125g (4oz; 1 cup) fresh peas
4 spring onions, sliced
2 carrots, diced
1 tsp grated ginger
1 tsp ground coriander
½ tsp ground turmeric
sea salt or kelp
coriander leaves for garnishing

Pour the stock into a saucepan and bring to the boil. Cut the chicken into thin strips and add to the pan to seal. Add the vegetables and spices and bring to the boil. Cover and simmer for 35 minutes.

Add the coconut milk and noodles and simmer for another 5 to 8 minutes, stirring occasionally. Garnish with chopped coriander leaves and serve.

Spanish omelette

4 free-range chicken eggs
1 onion, chopped
2 zucchini, thinly sliced
2 cloves garlic, crushed
2 tomatoes, skinned, seeded and chopped
1 tsp oregano
sea salt
2 tbsp olive oil

Warm the oil and a little water in a pan and cool-fry the onions until soft. Add the zucchini, garlic, tomatoes and seasoning, cover the pan and cook gently for 7 to 10 minutes.

Beat the eggs and stir into the vegetables. Cook over a gentle heat for 2 or 3 minutes until the underside is cooked. Place the pan under a preheated grill and cook the top of the omelette for another 2 or 3 minutes until set. Cut into quarters and serve.

Cold avocado and lime soup

3 ripe avocado pears
juice and zest of 3 limes
½ litre (1 pint; 2 cups) vegetable stock
sea salt
black pepper
chopped fresh chives for garnishing

Cut the avocado pears in half, remove the stones and scoop out the flesh. Place in a liquidizer, together with the lime juice and zest, and blend to a purée. Add the vegetable stock and seasoning, and serve cold garnished with chives.

Broccoli with ginger and macadamia nuts

450g (1lb; 4 cups) broccoli
1 tsp ginger, grated
50g (2oz; ½ cup) macadamia nuts, cut into slivers

Cut the broccoli into small pieces, separating the florets and cutting the stems into diagonal slices. Steam with the ginger for 3 or 4 minutes until soft but still bright green. Sprinkle with the nuts and serve with couscous or millet salad.

Couscous salad

225g (8oz; 1 cup) couscous (or quinoa)
½ litre (1 pint; 2 cups) boiling water
2 tomatoes, skinned and diced
1 small green pepper, diced
2 spring onions, finely sliced
juice of 1 lemon
freshly chopped basil or mint
sea salt
black pepper

Rinse the couscous in a fine-mesh strainer. Place in a bowl and pour on the hot water. Allow to stand for 15 minutes until the water has been absorbed. When cool, mix with the vegetables, herbs and seasoning. If using quinoa, cook in the boiling water for 20 minutes. When cool, mix with the vegetables, herbs and seasoning.

Day 28

You can now test **cows'** milk and **cows' milk products** –
yoghurt, cheese, cream, butter and ghee (clarified butter).
Clarified butter can often be tolerated by milk-sensitive
people. This is because the milk protein, traces of which are
found in butter, has been separated off. It can be bought as
ghee at Indian food shops and at most supermarkets. It can
also be made at home by melting a pack of butter over a
gentle heat, allowing it to cook slightly and then pouring off
the liquid into a glass jar. The proteins in the butter will then
have settled on the bottom of the pan.

Suggested menu

Breakfast: Fresh fruit with organic cows' milk yoghurt.
                Celebration carrot cake.
Main meal: Lamb noisettes with cheesy rice topping,
                garnished with mushrooms and served with
                seasonal green vegetables.
                Shepherd's pie (vegetarian or lamb), served with
                green vegetables.
Light meal: Minestrone soup.
                Baked potatoes with choice of fillings and fresh
                green salad.

Celebration carrot cake

175g (6oz; 1½ cups) wholemeal flour
125g (4oz; 1 cup) shredded carrot
250ml (½ pint; 1 cup) crushed pineapple and juice
125g (4oz; 1 cup) coconut
125g (4oz; 1 cup) walnuts, chopped
3 eggs, beaten
1 tsp cream of tartar
½ tsp bicarbonate of soda
125g (4oz; ½ cup) butter or oil
2 tsp cinnamon
2 tsp natural vanilla essence

Preheat the oven to 150°C (300°F), Gas Mark 2.

Mix all the ingredients together and place in a lined cake tin and bake for 40 minutes.

Lamb noisettes with cheesy rice topping

8 lamb cutlets, trimmed
grated cheese
FOR THE TOPPING:
1 large onion, chopped
50g (2oz; ½ cup) rice flakes
125ml (¼ pint; ½ cup) stock
knob of butter
sea salt
1 egg yolk
1 tbsp yoghurt

FOR THE GARNISH:
125g (4oz; 2 cups) mushrooms
1 tbsp mixed dried herbs (tarragon, mint, parsley)
sea salt

Preheat the oven to 160°C (310°F), Gas Mark 3.

To prepare the topping, place the rice, onion, salt and a knob of butter in a pan and pour over the stock. Bring to the boil and simmer for 35 minutes. Sieve the rice mixture and blend in the egg yolk and yoghurt to make a smooth purée.

Arrange the cutlets on a grill tray so that the bones all lie in the same direction. Grill the cutlets on one side only for about 5 minutes.

Carefully cover the cooked side of each cutlet with the purée. Sprinkle with grated cheese and arrange on a baking tray and cook in the oven for 20 minutes.

For the garnish, peel and trim the mushrooms. Chop the stalks and cool-fry in butter for about 1 minute without allowing the butter to brown. Add seasoning and herbs. Put the mixture into the hollow of the mushrooms and pour over a little melted butter. Place on a baking tray and cook in the oven for with the cutlets for 10 minutes.

Vegetarian or lamb shepherd's pie

225g (8oz; 1⅓ cups) brown lentils, sprouted and cooked
125g (4oz; ½ cup) buckwheat or pot barley, cooked
125g (4oz; 1 cup) chopped hazelnuts
(The lentils, buckwheat and hazelnuts may be replaced with
*   450g (1lb; 4 cups) of cooked, minced lamb.)*
2 onions, sliced
2 carrots, diced
1 stick celery, diced
1 zucchini, diced
tamari or teriyaki soya sauce
450g (1lb; 4 cups) potatoes, cooked and mashed
50g (2oz; ½ cup) Cheddar cheese (optional)

Preheat the oven to 160°C (310°F), Gas Mark 3.

Steam or boil the vegetables until tender. Mix with the lentils, buckwheat, hazelnuts (or lamb) and soya sauce and turn into a well-oiled ovenproof dish.

Top with the mashed potato, sprinkle with cheese and bake for 30 to 35 minutes.

Minestrone soup

450g (1lb; 4 cups) tomatoes, skinned and diced
1 potato, diced
125g (4oz; ⅔ cup) flageolet beans, sprouted and cooked
125g (4oz; 2 cups) wholemeal pasta shapes (wheat, barley,
*   millet or rice), cooked*
2 carrots, cut in half lengthways and sliced thinly
125g (4oz; 1 cup) green beans, cut into short pieces
1 zucchini, diced
50g (2oz; ½ cup) white cabbage, shredded
2 onions, chopped
2 cloves garlic, crushed
1 litre (1¾ pints; 4 cups) stock
2 bay leaves
2 tbsp fresh basil or oregano, chopped
sea salt
grated Parmesan cheese (optional)

Pour the stock into a pan and bring to the boil and add the potato, carrots, bay leaves first, followed by the tomatoes, green beans, zucchini, onions and garlic. Simmer for 20 minutes and then add the shredded cabbage, basil, flageolet beans, seasoning and pasta and cook for a further 2 or 3 minutes.

Remove the bay leaves and serve with Parmesan cheese.

Stuffed baked potatoes

Preheat the oven to 190°C (375°F), Gas Mark 5.

Scrub the potatoes and prick all over with a fork. Bake for about 1 hour until tender.

Remove the potatoes from the oven, cut a cross in the top, press open and scoop out some of the soft centre, placing it in a bowl. Mash with a filling and pile the mixture back into the potato and return to the oven for a further 10 minutes to heat through.

Suitable fillings include the following:

- fromage frais, celery and chives
- Cheddar cheese, mushrooms (chopped and cooked) and thyme
- tuna with sweetcorn relish (see page 120)
- salmon with tomato relish (see page 120)
- Cheddar cheese and date and apple chutney (see page 120).

Sweetcorn relish

225g (8oz; 2 cups) sweetcorn
1 red pepper, de-seeded and chopped
½ cucumber, diced
¼ tsp chilli powder (optional)
½ tsp ground mustard
black pepper
sea salt

Place half the sweetcorn in a liquidizer and blend. Mix with the remaining ingredients and the rest of the corn.

Tomato relish

225g (8oz; 2 cups) tomatoes, skinned, de-seeded and chopped
4 spring onions, chopped
50g (2oz; ½ cup) capers
1 stick celery, chopped
paprika pepper
1 tbsp tomato purée
freshly chopped basil
pinch of allspice
sea salt

Mix the ingredients together and use as required.

Date and apple chutney

225g (8oz; 2 cups) eating apples, chopped
225g (8oz; 2 cups) cooking apples, chopped
225g (8oz; 2 cups) stoned dates, chopped
225g (8oz; 2 cups) sultanas
225g (8oz; 2 cups) onions, chopped
250ml (½ pint; 1 cup) cider vinegar
125g (4oz; ½ cup) raw cane molasses sugar (optional)
1 tsp grated ginger
pinch of allspice
sea salt

Bring the vinegar to the boil and add all the ingredients. Cook for 15 to 20 minutes until tender and the cooking apples have become mushy.

The chutney can be bottled, refrigerated or frozen.

CHAPTER 5

The Next Step

Now you have discovered which foods you are reacting to, you can simply avoid these items so that your system can have a rest. In this way it will have a chance to recover and re-balance. You may want to make a list of all the foods you have had a reaction to and note the severity of the reaction. If the reaction was only a minor one, you may find that you can eat the food on an occasional basis, perhaps once a week, or in a rotation diet. Foods which cause major reactions, though, will need to be avoided for two to three months before being tested again.

A rotation diet is a way of ensuring that your body can clear itself of each food before it is eaten again. The basic idea is to give your body at least three days to metabolize each food. This can prevent you from reacting to any more foods and can also relieve any existing intolerances. *The Rotation Diet Cookbook* shows you how to follow such a diet, as well as providing you with recipes for each day.

You can also help your body to recover by strengthening your immune system. A strong immune system will be able to fight off viruses, bacteria and other organisms and protect you from radiation, chemical pollution and all other toxic and poisonous substances far more effectively. This in turn will give your body more of a chance to re-balance, thus making any reactions less and less severe.

Supplements

Deficiencies in vitamins or minerals can have a debilitating effect on the immune system, so it is important to eat good, nourishing food. Additional food supplements may also be necessary, especially when many foods need to be eliminated or when the nutrients in the foods are not being absorbed properly, which is often the case with allergy sufferers. However, it would be wise to consult a health practitioner before embarking on a programme of supplements so that you do not waste money buying supplements of poor quality or ones which may cause adverse reactions. He or she will also be able to advise you on quantities. The following supplements may be prescribed and may prove to be useful.

- Digestive enzymes: these can help break down undigested food components such as proteins. They consist of hydrochloric acid and pepsin, normally present in the stomach, and pancreatic enzymes normally present in the duodenum and small intestines. An alternative is to eat more raw food as the enzymes in the food will not have been destroyed by cooking.

- Probiotics: these are a way of re-colonizing good bacteria that may have been destroyed by drugs or poor diet. If harmful bacteria are allowed to take over, it can lead to conditions such as candidiasis. However, care needs to be taken in choosing a good quality supplement which contains *Lactobacillus acidophilus* and *Bifidobacterium*, either separately or together. Capsules should be bought in vacuum-sealed bottles and, once opened, kept in the refrigerator.

- Soluble fibre: this helps to speed up the transport of food through the intestines. The longer poorly digested food stays in the gut, the more likely it is to cause problems. Fibre also helps to clean the walls of the intestines. The best sources are oat bran, rice bran, pectin and physillium husks.

- Essential fatty acids: these are vital for the immune system, and for the health and protection of the gastro-intestinal mucosa and the cell membranes throughout the body. The essential fatty acids are omega-3-alpha linolenic acid and omega-6-linoleic acid. Flax seed oil is one of the best and richest sources of omega-3. This is also present in soya bean, walnut and wheatgerm oils. Omega-6 EFAs are found in sesame seed, safflower, sunflower, corn and evening primrose oils. These oils should be unrefined and cold-pressed and kept refrigerated once opened, as oils can become rancid quite quickly and in this state they can affect the body adversely. Deficiency can result in stunted growth, hair loss, varicose veins, brittle nails, sexual immaturity, nervousness and skin disorders – especially eczema and dandruff.

- Multi-minerals and vitamins: these may be necessary as it is increasingly difficult to obtain all the necessary amounts from foods alone.

- Antioxidants: these include vitamins A, C and E, selenium, zinc, L-Cysteine and L-Glutathione. Apart from being important nutrients, these vitamins and minerals protect cells against harmful free radicals. A free radical is an atom or molecule with an unpaired electron. It can be extremely damaging because it attempts to pair its free electron with an electron from neighbouring molecules and can then set up a chain reaction causing damage to further cells. This 'latching-on' process is called oxidation and can 'rust' the body almost as it does metal. Free radicals form because people are being exposed to thousands of substances, alien to the human body, such as atmospheric pollution, pesticides, additives, tobacco, alcohol, and many forms of medicines. Radiation and hard physical exercise are also contributory factors. Unsaturated fats which are found naturally in cell membranes are particularly susceptible to free radical damage. The cell walls then become vulnerable to cancer, arteriosclerosis, arthritis, premature ageing and other diseases.

- Vitamin C: this also has natural anti-inflammatory properties and is important for iron absorption and in the production of collagen, a protein necessary for the formation of connective tissue in the skin, ligaments and bones. It also helps to control blood cholesterol levels and is an anti-stress factor. Deficiency may show itself in swollen gums, weakened enamel or dentine, sore joints, fatigue, lowered resistance to infection, nosebleeds, slow healing of wounds and a poor complexion.

- Ginkgo biloba: this is a herb which is also a powerful antioxidant and a useful protector for the intestinal mucosa. It improves the blood circulation in the hands, legs, feet and in the brain, thus improving memory and concentration.

- The B vitamins: this is a group of vitamins which is essential for the release of energy from food and vital for the metabolism of proteins and fats. They help maintain a good circulation and healthy skin, hair and eyes. They contribute to the functioning of the brain and nervous system, to maintaining the correct balance of hormones in the body and to increasing one's ability to deal with stress.

- Magnesium: this is needed for the metabolism of carbohydrates to release energy, for nerve impulse transmission and brain function and for normal muscle function including that of the heart. Symptoms of deficiency may include apprehensiveness, muscle twitches, tremors, confusion and forgetfulness, sleeplessness and the formation of clots in the heart and brain, and may contribute to calcium deposits in the kidneys, blood vessels and heart. As soil and hence the vegetable levels of magnesium are low, most of us could do with a supplement.

- Iodine: this aids in the development and functioning of the thyroid gland, being a chief constituent of thyroxin, a principle hormone, and is particularly important for children and the elderly. Iodine plays an important role in regulating the body's production of energy, and it stimulates the rate of metabolism, helping the body to burn off excess fat. Mental alertness, clear speech and the condition of the hair, nails, skin and teeth are dependent upon a well functioning thyroid gland. Iodine is necessary for neutralizing certain toxic substances and for protecting the body from the harmful effects of radiation. It is found in seaweed or can be taken in the form of kelp powder or tablets.

- Zinc: this is necessary for the production of a vast number of enzymes and hormones present in the body. This is also a mineral which has become very depleted in the soil. Stretch marks in the skin and white spots on the nails can be a sign of zinc deficiency. It may also produce an increase in fatigue, susceptibility to infection and a decrease in mental alertness.

Enhancing our lifestyle

In addition to diet and nutrition, we need to look at other aspects of our lives in order to strengthen our immune system and receive the benefits of good health. This includes getting sufficient exercise, fresh air and sunlight, learning to relax, improving our posture and breathing habits, and, above all, enhancing the quality of our thoughts.

Relaxation

Some people manage to be easy-going and relaxed, no matter what the stresses and pressures on them. For others, even a small problem becomes a major disaster and a source of constant worry, anger or anxiety. Strong emotions affect the physical body, causing muscle tension and upsetting our hormonal balance; so learning to relax is a vital ingredient to getting well and ultimately to finding our true self. The following practices can help.

- Neck rolls and shoulder lifts: either standing or sitting, take four deep breaths and then slowly turn your head to one side and then to the other and repeat four times. Next, tip your head forwards and back four times, then rotate four times, first one way and then the other. Next, lift your shoulders up towards your neck, hold for the count of four and drop. Do this four or five times.

- Muscle relaxation exercises: take a few moments to lie down, preferably on a hard surface. Close your eyes and, starting with your feet and working up through your body, tense each part of your body as much as you can, hold for a few seconds and then relax. Then tense your entire body, screw up your face and then completely relax.

- Meditation: there are many meditation techniques, but all of them aim to bring about a state of tranquillity by stilling the mind and letting distracting thoughts and worries drift away. We cannot underestimate the power of the mind – it can be our greatest enemy, but also our strongest ally, and our thoughts of today create our reality tomorrow. There are many groups which teach meditation or you can try the following method. Choose a quiet room, sit in an upright but comfortable chair, and close your eyes. Do a few neck rolls and shoulder lifts and take a few deep breaths, sighing and relaxing as you exhale. Choose a word or phrase that has no negative emotional connotations for you such as the word 'one' or 'peace'. Repeat the word silently to yourself without moving your lips. If any thoughts or images enter your mind, just allow them to float away while you keep your attention on your chosen word. You can start by doing this for 5 minutes twice a day, gradually building up to 20 minutes. Some people may choose to focus on a visual object such as a flower, candle or a mandala.

Visualization

This is the art of using one's imagination to produce positive changes. By learning how to see something happening as a 'picture' in your mind, you can gain considerable relief from your symptoms. For example, if you have a pain in your muscles or joints, or toothache, you need to visualize the painful area and 'see' the pain going away.

The inner smile is a powerful tool for self-healing which uses the healing power of visualization to enhance the health of all the organs and parts of the body.

Exercise

Whether we choose an aerobic activity which aims to raise our heart rate, yoga-type stretching exercises or a brisk walk every day, our bodies are designed to move and our increasingly sedentary lifestyles can take their toll. Exercise strengthens and tones the muscles of the body, increases blood and lymphatic circulation and the elimination of toxic waste through perspiration, strengthens the lungs' ability to transport oxygen to the heart and carbon dioxide and waste from it, increases the metabolic rate, releases pent-up emotions, helps one sleep better and generally makes one feel stronger, healthier and more confident.

Valuing our health

We owe it to ourselves to be well. If we are well, we have energy, vitality, and are a joy to be with. Health also gives us the ability to work and achieve our aims in life.

Perhaps we think that by ignoring problems, they will go away. However, we all know how much easier it is if we nip things in the bud. Think of a dandelion growing out of place in a herbaceous border – when it first shows a couple of leaves it only takes a finger and thumb to remove it; leave it and the roots grow deeper until a garden spade and a surgical operation is needed to remove it, damaging surrounding flowers and plants in the procedure. We need to take heed of our own early warning signs.

It is now widely accepted that what we eat and how we prepare and cook our food can have an enormous effect on our health. You will have seen how one bite of a sandwich, or one sip of a drink can affect your entire body, both physically and mentally. But you will also have seen how to use food to your benefit. The choice is now up to you. Advances in transport and food distribution have brought an increasing abundance and array of fruits, vegetables and all kinds of different foods to our shops. So go out and experiment; say goodbye to the foods which can cause you problems – the 'convenience' foods full of additives; wheat, corn and dairy products; the fizzy drinks full of sugar; the chocolate and the potato chips. Instead, let your innate wisdom guide you to the right foods for you.

Working with the Elimination Diet can be a valuable way of getting to know yourself; knowing what your body needs and gradually becoming more 'in tune' with yourself and therefore with everything else in your life.

Mary, aged 49, was bothered by a lot of symptoms. She was overweight, and suffered from itching skin, tingling in her legs, weeping eyes, sensitivity to bright lights, hot flushes, palpitations, water retention, bloating, thrush, backache, pain in her muscles and joints, poor sleep, tension, anxiety, forgetfulness, difficulty in making decisions, aggressiveness and hyperactivity; she was constantly snacking, craving particular foods and had little desire for sex. Mary went to see a nutritionist who believed that many of these symptoms might decrease if she changed her diet. Mary was found to be reacting to several foods: all dairy produce, potatoes, tomatoes, tea and peanuts, as well as the sprays on foods. After four months of avoiding these foods, most of the symptoms had disappeared. Her head and eyes felt clearer than they had for years, her mood swings became a thing of the past and her crippling backache and other pains vanished. However, she still felt some anxiety. The hot flushes continued, as did the tingling in her legs and she was still overweight. Her practitioner then suggested she take a vitamin and mineral test to see how many deficiencies she had. It was discovered that Mary needed magnesium supplements, also zinc, selenium, iron and vitamins C, B1, B2, B3 and B5. Her weight now is rapidly reducing, tingling in her legs no longer occurs, she is much less anxious and the hot flushes have almost disappeared. After years of misery, Mary is discovering what it is like to feel good again.

Appendix I

Weights and measures

Metric and Imperial measures have been given in this book. The recipes refer to Imperial pints as used in the UK and Australia which contain 20 fl oz. The American pint, on the other hand, contains 16 fl oz. Cups refer to the American 8 fl oz measuring cup.

A teaspoon is standard at approximately 5 ml. Tablespoons, however, do vary. The measures given in this book refer to the UK standard, ie 17.7 ml. The table below gives a conversion chart.

UK	American	Australian
17.7 ml	14.2 ml	20 ml
1 tablespoon	1 tablespoon	1 tablespoon
2 tablespoons	3 tablespoons	2 tablespoons
3½ tablespoons	4 tablespoons	3 tablespoons
4 tablespoons	5 tablespoons	3½ tablespoons

Appendix II

Food ingredients

Foods containing wheat:
wheat flour
wheat bran
wheatmeal
wheat-based crispbreads
wheat biscuits
wheat breakfast cereals (All-
    bran Weetabix, Puffed Wheat,
    muesli)
modified starch
baking powder
thickeners and binders
bakery products
some pumpernickel bread
cakes and cake mixes
batter mixes
spaghetti
macaroni and other pasta
pastry
mustard
**also check the ingredients of
the following:**
baked beans
chocolate and other sweets
cocoa
instant coffee
imitation cream
custard
instant puddings
spreads and pastes
some other flours, eg rice flour
bean flours

buckwheat pasta
rye bread
sausages
beefburgers
hamburgers
corned beef
salami
luncheon meat
pâtés
foods coated in breadcrumbs or
    batter
canned soups
sauces
stock cubes
gravy
white sauce
soya sauce
chutneys
alcoholic drinks – whisky, most
    gins, lager, ale, beer, some
    wines
vitamin and mineral tablets

**Foods containing milk and
dairy products:**
cows', goats' and sheep's milk
condensed milk
dried milk
evaporated milk
skimmed and powdered milk
butter
buttermilk

cream
cheese including dishes cooked
  with cheese
whey
lactose
casinates
margarines (check whey on
  labels)
yoghurts
custards
biscuits
cakes
ice-cream
foods cooked in batter
soups
sauces
sausages
prepared meats
most packets of convenience
  foods
some vitamin and mineral
  tablets

Homoeopathic remedies can be
obtained in a liquid form free
from sucrose and lactose;
doctors can contact
manufacturers to find
pain-relieving medicines which
are milk-free – most tablets
contain lactose.

**Foods and products
containing corn:**
adhesives
envelopes
stamps
stickers
lining of cans for vegetables
lining of paper plates and dishes
toothpaste
talcum powders
laundry starch
aspirin and other tablets
cough syrups

cornflower
sweetcorn
popcorn
biscuits
candies
instant coffee and tea
custard
instant whip puddings
ice-cream
cornflakes
ales, beers, whisky and some
  wines
fizzy drinks
batters for frying
corn or maize oil
margarines containing maize oil
peanut butter
salad dressings
bleached white flour
powdered sugar
jam
milk in paper cartons
canned beans and peas
some brands of crisps
corn snacks
tortillas
gravy mixes and cubes
sausages
bacon
cured and tenderized ham
creamed soups
stuffing
glucose syrup and glucose in
  jams
monosodium glutamate
  (Chinese foods)
distilled vinegar
soya sauce
tomato sauce
salt-shakers in cafés
pie fillings
fruit juices
canned and frozen fruits
soya bean milks

boiled sweets
chewing gum
vitamin C is derived from corn

Foods containing eggs:
buns
croissants
Danish pastries
biscuits
cakes
flans
pastries and pies
salad dressings and salad cream
mayonnaise
some prepared salads
custard powder
ice-creams
lemon curd
instant whips and processed
   cream preparations
egg white in meringues
macaroons
marshmallows
sorbets
consommé soups
frostings and royal icings
batter mixes made with egg
quiches
fishcakes
egg pasta
enriched alcoholic drinks (egg-
   nogs)
many vaccines are grown on egg
   and may cause reactions

Foods which contain yeast:
breads
some biscuits
crispbreads
cakes and cake mixes
flour enriched with vitamins
   from yeast
food coated in breadcrumbs

some milk powders are fortified
   with vitamins from yeast (B
   vitamins)
mushrooms
truffles
cheese of all kinds
buttermilk and cottage cheese
vinegar and all convenience
   foods containing vinegar
gravy browning and similar
   extracts
yeast/beef extracts
stock cubes
fermented drinks – whisky, gin,
   wine, brandy, rum, vodka,
   beer, etc
malted products
cereals
sweets and chocolates
milk drinks which have been
   malted.
citrus fruit juice (only home
   squeezed are yeast free)
many B vitamins products are
   derived from yeast

Foods which contain sugar:
most alcoholic drinks
bakery products except
   stoneground wholemeal bread
instant coffee and tea
drinking chocolate
malted milk drinks
milk shakes
soft drinks and low calorie
   drinks
fruit juices and squashes except
   pure fruit juices
most breakfast cereals
most pre-cooked oven ready
   foods
milk products, eg baby milks
cream, whipped cream, ice-
   cream

processed cheeses
some fruit yoghurts
many frozen and packages
  foods
many jams
some honey may have sucrose
  added to it
sauces, eg tomato sauce
soya and other oriental sauces

mayonnaise
relishes
all sweets and candies
all tinned vegetables
fruits
soups
sauces
desserts are likely to contain
  sugar

Appendix III

The Elimination Diet at a glance

DAY 1	DAY 2	DAY3	DAY 4
Rice	Rice	Rice	Rice
Pears	Pears	Pears	Pears
Lamb or lentils	Lamb or lentils	Lamb or lentils	Lamb or lentils
		Equisetum tea	Linden leaf tea

DAY 8	DAY 9	DAY 10	DAY 11
Sago	Rice	Barley	Quail, Quails'
Sorghum	Lamb	Fish: saltwater	eggs
Yam	Tap water	Venison	Lily family
Rabbit, hare	Pea family (not	Beet family	Laurel family
Aster family	soya)	Olives	Citrus family
Plum family	Pears, quince,	Rose family	Blueberry
Sunflower oil	loquat	Conifer family	family
Safflower oil	Lychees	Pumpkin seeds	Chestnuts
Almond oil	Brazil nuts	Mulberry family	Birch family
Honey	Macadamia	Cashew family	Orange juice
Camomile tea	nuts	Lemon grass	Rice syrup
	Lemon verbena	tea	
	tea	Raspberry leaf	
	Fenugreek tea	tea	

DAY 15	DAY 16	DAY 17	DAY 18
Turkey	Corn	Yeast	Rye
Rooibosch tea	Chicory coffee	Green leaf tea	Fish:
Myrtle family	Dandelion		crustacean
Black and white	coffee		family
pepper	Barleycup		
Quails' eggs			

DAY 22	DAY 23	DAY 24	DAY 25
Wheat, spelt	Chicken	Goats' milk	Tea
wheat, kamut	Chickens' eggs	products	Peanuts
Fish: mollusc			Cider vinegar
family			

DAY 5
Rice
Lamb
Lentils
Mustard family
Kiwi fruit
Flax seed oil
  (linseed)

DAY 6
Quinoa
Fish: oily
  saltwater
Sweet potato
Arum family
Mallow family
Melon family
Gooseberry
  family
Olive oil
Mint family tea
Fruit sugar

DAY 7
Buckwheat
  family
Millet, tapioca
Game bird
Walnut family
Tiger nuts
Parsley family
Banana family
Pineapple,
  papaya
Walnut oil
Fennel tea
Maple syrup

DAY 12
Beef and veal
Potato family
Grape family
Seaweed
Plam family
Sesame seeds
  and oil
Date syrup
Barley

DAY 13
Pork, wild boar
Soya products
Mushrooms
Apples, pectin
Mustard seed

DAY 14
Oats
Fish: freshwater
Ginger family
Nutmeg family

DAY 19
Duck, goose
Ducks' eggs,
  goose eggs

DAY 20
Sheep's milk
  products

DAY 21
Cane sugar
Wine vinegar

DAY 26
Cocoa
Vanilla

DAY 27
Coffee

DAY 28
Cows' milk
  products

Useful Addresses

AUSTRALIA

Allergy Association Australia
PO Box 298
Ringwood
Victoria 3134

Allergy Recognition and Management
PO Box 2
Sandy Bay
Tasmania 7005

Australian Natural Therapists Association
PO Box 308
Melrose Park
South Australia 5039
Tel 8297 9533
Fax 8297 0003

CANADA

AIA Allergy Information Association
3 Powburn Place
Weston
Ontario

IRELAND

Irish Allergy Association
PO Box 1067
Churchtown
Dublin

NEW ZEALAND

Allergy Awareness Association
PO Box 120701
Penrose
Auckland 6
New Zealand

New Zealand Natural Health Practitioners Accreditation Board
PO Box 37–491
Auckland
New Zealand
Tel 9 625 9966
Supported by 15 therapy organizations

UNITED KINGDOM

Action Against Allergy
43 The Downs
London SW20

British Digestive Foundation
3 St Andrew's Place
London NW1 4LB
Tel 0171 487 5332

British Homeopathic Association
27a Devonshire Street
London W1N 1RJ
Tel 0171 935 2163
Medically qualified homeopaths only

British Society for Nutritional Medicine
Stone House
9 Weymouth Street
London W1N 3FF
Tel 0171 436 8532

The General Council and Register of Naturopaths
6 Netherall Gardens
London NW3

The Institute for Optimum Nutrition
Blades Court
Deodar Road
London SW15 2NU

Society for the Promotion of Nutritional Therapy (SPNT)
PO Box 47
Heathfields
East Sussex
TN21 8ZX

USA

Allergy Foundation of America
801 Second Avenue
New York 10017

American Association of Naturopathic Physicians
2800 East Madison Street
Suite 200
Seattle
Washington 98112
or
PO Box 20386
Seattle
Washington 98102
Tel 206 323 7610
Fax 206 323 7612

International Academy of Environmental Medicine
Prairie Village
Kansas
Tel 913 642 6062

Internal Academy of Nutrition and Preventative Medicine
PO Box 5832
Lincoln
Nebraska 68505
Tel 402 467 2716

Further Reading

Bloomfield, B, *The Mystique of Healing*, Skilton & Shaw, Edinburgh, 1984

Brostoff, Dr J and Gamlin, L, *Food Allergy and Intolerance*, Bloomsbury, London, 1989

Budd, Martin, *Low Blood Sugar*, Thorsons, London, 1995

Carter, Jill, and Alison Edwards, *The Rotation Diet Cookbook*, Element Books, Shaftesbury, England, 1997

Chia, Manta K, *Awaken Healing Energy through the Tao*, Aurora Press, 1983

Davies, Gwynne, *Overcoming Food Allergies*, Ashgrove, Bath, England, 1985

Davies, Dr S and Stewart, Dr A, *Nutritional Medicine*, Pan Books, London, 1987

Dong, Dr, *New Hope for the Arthritic*, Granada Press, St Albans, England, 1980

Erasmus, Udo, *Fats that Heal, Fats that Kill*, Alive Books, Burnaby, Canada, 1993

Galland, Dr L, *Allergy Prevention for Kids*, Bloomsbury, London, 1989

Lewith, Dr G, Kenyon, Dr J and Dowson, Dr D, *Allergy and Intolerance*, Merlin Press, London, 1992

Mackarness, R, *Chemical Victims*, Pan, London, 1980

Mackarness, R, *Not all in the Mind*, Pan, London, 1976

Mansfield, Dr P and Munro, Dr J, *Chemical Children*, Century Paperbacks, London, 1987

Mental and Elemental Nutrients, Brain Bio Centre, Princetown, New Jersey, USA, 1975

Needes, R, *You Don't Have To Feel Unwell*, Gateway, Bath, England, 1984

Randolph, T and Moss, R, *Allergies: Your Hidden Enemy*, Turnstone, Wellingborough, England, 1981

Rapp, Doris J, *Allergies and the Hyperactive Child*, Sterling Publishing, New York, 1988

Schause, A, *Diet, Crime & Delinquency*, Parker House, Berkeley, USA, 1980

General Index

Index of Foods and Recipes

The 'day' references indicates the day on which the food is introduced and/or tested. Recipes are also given in italic where the food is an important ingredient.